THERAPY WITH REMARRIAGE FAMILIES

James C. Hansen, Editor
Lillian Messinger, Volume Editor

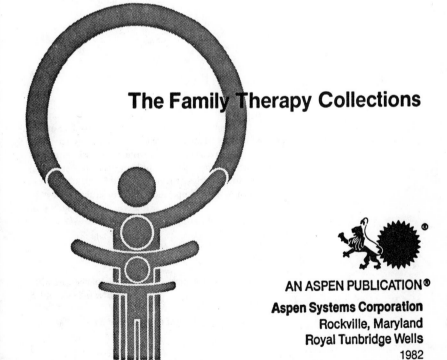

The Family Therapy Collections

AN ASPEN PUBLICATION®

Aspen Systems Corporation
Rockville, Maryland
Royal Tunbridge Wells
1982

Library of Congress Cataloging in Publication Data
Main entry under title:

Therapy with remarriage families·

(The Family therapy collections
Includes bibliographical references·
1. Family psychotherapy·
2. Remarriage—Psychological aspects·
I. Messinger, Lillian   II. Hansen, James C.   III. Series
RC488.5.T49   616.89'156   82-6799
             ISBN 0-89443-601-5   AACR2

Publisher· John Marozsan
Managing Editor: Margot Raphael
Printing and Manufacturing· Debbie Swarr

Library of Congress Catalog Card Number: 82-6799
ISBN. 0-89443-601-5

Printed in the United States of America

2   3   4   5

Table of Contents

Board of Editors

Contributors

Volume Editor

LILLIAN MESSINGER
Clarke Institute of Psychiatry
Toronto, Ontario, Canada

CONSTANCE R. AHRONS
School of Social Work
University of Wisconsin-Madison
Wisconsin Family Studies Institute
Madison, Wisconsin

JOYCE AMBLER
Texas Research Institute
of Mental Sciences
Houston, Texas

MARIO D. BARTOLETTI
Bartoletti Consultants
Scarborough, Ontario, Canada

PATRICIA BOURKE
Bartoletti Consultants
Scarborough, Ontario, Canada

CAROL ANN BRADY
Texas Research Institute
of Mental Sciences
Houston, Texas

HOLLY BROWN
Jewish Board of Family and
Children's Services
New York, New York

HELEN CROHN
Jewish Board of Family and
Children's Services
New York, New York

ROBERT GARFIELD
Hahneman Medical College and
Hospital
Philadelphia, Pennsylvania

LAWRENCE D. GAUGHAN
Attorney-at-Law
Arlington, Virginia

VIRGINIA GOLDNER
Albert Einstein College of
Medicine
New York, New York

JUDITH BROWN GREIF
Division of Child and Adolescent
Psychiatry
Albert Einstein College
of Medicine
New York, New York

DOROTHY S. HUNTINGTON
Center for the Family
in Transition
Corte Madera, California

MARLA BETH ISAACS
Families of Divorce Project
Philadelphia Child Guidance
Clinic
Philadelphia, Pennsylvania

Contributors
(continued)

ELLEN M. MACDONALD
Bartoletti Consultants
Scarborough, Ontario, Canada

MORTON S. PERLMUTTER
School of Social Work
University of Wisconsin-Madison
Wisconsin Family Studies Institute
Madison, Wisconsin

BONNIE ROBSON
C.M. Hincks Treatment Centre
Toronto, Ontario, Canada

EVELYN RODSTEIN
Jewish Board of Family and
Children's Services
New York, New York

CLIFFORD J. SAGER
Jewish Board of Family and
Children's Services
New York, New York

EMILY B. VISHER
Stepfamily Association of America
Palo Alto, California

JOHN S. VISHER
Adult Outpatient Services
North County Mental Health
Center
Palo Alto, California

LIBBY WALKER
Jewish Board of Family and
Children's Services
New York, New York

Preface

THE FAMILY THERAPY COLLECTIONS IS A SERIES OF PUB-
lications reviewing topics of current and specific interest and translating
theory and research into practical applications. *The Family Therapy Collections* serves as a source of information for the practicing professional
by gathering, synthesizing, and applying the research and literature of the
field. Each volume of *The Family Therapy Collections* contains a collection of articles, each authored by one or more practicing professionals,
providing in-depth coverage of a single significant aspect of family therapy. The collection of the many volumes covers the body of professional
practice literature.

This volume of *The Family Therapy Collections* concentrates on therapy with the remarriage family. Remarriage families are often also called
reconstituted families, blended families, or stepfamilies. With the increasing number of divorces, therapists encounter people in various
stages of separation, in various individual and partial family living arrangements, and in the process of remarrying. Each stage presents concerns for adults and children. This volume provides the therapist with
knowledge and techniques useful in helping the family members. Several
articles explore the concerns and needs of children and adults in dealing
with the loss inherent in the separation process. Successful coping at this
stage helps the adjustment in reconstituting a family. The remaining
articles offer concepts and techniques in assisting the remarrying family
resolve their problems.

Lillian Messinger, the volume editor, is chief social worker, Community Resources Section, Clarke Institute of Psychiatry, Toronto, and on

staff in the Department of Psychiatry, University of Toronto. She was the principal investigator of the Remarriage Research Project, one of the earliest research projects revealing the complexities of the remarriage family. Therapists have discovered the significance of this work and she has also received wide recognition for her numerous publications, professional programs, and workshops on the remarriage family. Her research and clinical experience have provided her the breadth of knowledge to identify appropriate topics and to select authors with the specific expertise.

This volume is an outstanding accumulation of knowledge collected for the therapist working with families during the separation and remarriage processes. The reader will find it useful in developing an orientation for working with remarried families. It will long continue to be a valuable resource.

James C. Hansen
Editor

Introduction

THIS VOLUME DEALS WITH THE GROWING POPULATION OF families in remarriage following divorce. Since the liberalization of the Divorce Act in 1968, the inclusion of the marriage breakdown clause enabled many couples whose marriage had broken down to legalize their divorce and consequently to remarry. Over three fourths of the divorced persons remarry within 3–5 years of their divorce (Norton & Glick, 1976). The unprecedented increase in divorce and remarriage is well documented.

By 1978, the number of divorces granted in the United States was close to half the number of marriages (U.S. National Center for Health Statistics, 1979). Over half the divorces involved minor children, with over 1,123,000 children experiencing parental divorce. The rate of divorce has continued to rise steadily. It is estimated that nearly 40% of children born around 1970 will live in a one-parent or remarriage family at some point during their first 18 years (Bane, 1976).

In Duberman's (1975) study of the future of marriage, the prognostication is that more people will be living in a second marriage than in a first marriage by the end of this century. This would suggest that most of us, both in our personal and our professional lives, will have close contact with persons who have divorced and remarried. Despite the extent of this different family system, it is a significant fact that remarriage remains poorly institutionalized.

This statistical picture conveys the message that there is a large population living in a family system different from that with which we have been familiar. Remarriages may now and in the future serve some basic functions of family life; however, the varieties of remarriage structures pose problems of adaptation for which earlier socialization in the nuclear family provides an inadequate model. A conceptual model is required that can reflect the various structures of remarriage in order to depathologize the system and constitute a normal range of functioning appropriate to a legally reconstituted family. The remarriage family system is distinct from the first intact family in terms of basic theoretical concepts. Society continues to assume that the normal course for the typical family will run from birth to death and will include courtship, till-death-do-us-part marriage, parenthood, and other traditional roles

I began to study remarriage about 1974, by which time a new client population had begun to emerge. Couples in their second marriage with children from the previous marriage were seeking help with problems that they were experiencing while trying to bring a sense of family integration to the new group (with a different cast of actors) and with few cues to go by. The problems with which they were presented had a different focus than first marriage and family problems. To identify the particular areas of stress that people in second marriages experience, a team at Clarke Institute of Psychiatry, Toronto, embarked on a research project. We administered questionnaires, held in-depth interviews, and ran group seminars with remarried couples and later with multi-remarried family groups. There were consistent findings that indicated that remarriage has complexities that people had not been aware of and for which they were not prepared. The interviews and group discussions revealed that problems that burden remarriage are frequently tied in with unresolved problems from the first marriage. These focused on the relationships between ex-spouses and management of the transitional tasks from the marriage breakdown through the separated–divorced stages, as well as poor resolution for the children regarding the family disorganization and loss of one parent from the family home. The concerns that related to personal and family emotional problems were exacerbated by pressures from external forces, such as the legal divorce process that lagged behind behavioral needs. Our research and clinical experience led us to believe that lack of personal, social, and legislative recognition of remarriage as a unique family arrangement are the major causes for unrealistic expectations and disappointments that the couples and the remarriage household experience.

The remarriage family has its roots in the original family. Awareness of the process by which the remarriage family evolves is crucial to the understanding and appreciation of the difficulties involved for the new group to be able to integrate with a sense of family unity. The traditional concepts for family integration and family unity must be reassessed. The remarriage family lacks the autonomy and sense of family identity that is attributed to first marriage. Remarriage family roles differ from nuclear family roles in the degree of clarity, the rights, and the obligations. The remarriage family lacks the history of shared life events and tradition that creates the sense of belonging in the nuclear family. Given the absence of socially defined roles appropriate to the stepparent–stepchild situation, the expectation that the nuclear family model can be juxtaposed on the legally reconstituted family is unrealistic. Furthermore, our culturally defined kinship relations refer to blood ties, not social ties. To help facilitate the remarriage family as an established mode of family life with a public image and with appropriate role expectations corresponding to its reality, further research is needed to examine the steps that can reduce the stress in remarriage following divorce.

I am grateful to the authors who have contributed their expertise to further our understanding about this different and complex family system. Their articles convey the message that remarriage cannot be viewed as a separate life event; rather, it is an integrated totality of our human experiences. It is imperative to deal with the separation from the first family as part of the remarriage. As Minuchin (1974) states, "the individual's present is his past plus his current circumstances. Part of his past will always survive" (p.14).

The contents of the volume have been arranged in temporal sequence to be consistent with the remarriage cycle. The therapist would be well advised to perceive the complete process from the period of separation, through the issues involved in living apart as a continuum with the plans to reconstitute a family, to fully understand problems that may occur in remarriage.

The first group of articles deals with problems that people experience in the separation process. It is important to focus considerable attention on this phase because it has such an impact on the remarriage. Garfield, in the first article, describes the grieving process for couples who separate. Huntington emphasizes the importance of the loss of attachment that is involved in divorce. Ahrons and Perlmutter describe the issues in ex-spouse relations. Greif focuses on the concerns in father–child relations after separation and divorce. Robson presents a developmental understanding and treatment suggestions for working with children.

Two articles concentrate attention on some of the legal practices and some alternatives to the prevailing adversarial system. Bartoletti, Bourke, and Macdonald propose a joint legal and marital counseling alternative, and Gaughan describes a divorce mediation process.

The Vishers present an overview to the issues facing stepfamilies in the 1980s and to the areas of therapeutic intervention. Isaacs outlines the major problems in restructuring the remarried families and illustrates therapeutic techniques for each. Brady and Ambler share their program and research using group techniques with remarried couples. Crohn, Sager, Brown, Engel, Rodstein, and Walker present their model for understanding and treating remarried families. In the final article, Goldner takes a global look at changing family patterns in the 1980s.

The authors have drawn on their distinguished extensive professional research and clinical experience presenting alternatives to present practices. There are many unanswered areas that require further exploration. If this volume helps the practicing professional working with remarriage families and stimulates further thought and research, it will have made a significant contribution toward stabilizing remarriage as a family life style.

REFERENCES

Bane, M. *Here to stay: American families in twentieth century.* New York: Basic Books, 1976.

Duberman, L. *The reconstituted family: A study of remarried couples and their children.* Chicago: Nelson-Hall, 1975.

Minuchin, S. *Families and family therapy.* Cambridge, Mass.: Harvard University Press, 1974.

Norton, A.J., & Glick, P.C. Marital instability: Past, present and future. *Journal of Social Issues,* 1976, *32*(1), 5–20.

U.S. National Center for Health Statistics 1979—Monthly Vital Statistics Report 27(12). Washington, D.C.: U.S. Government Printing Office.

Lillian Messinger
Clarke Institute of Psychiatry
Volume Editor

1. Mourning and Its Resolution for Spouses in Marital Separation

Robert Garfield, M.D.
Hahneman Medical College and Hospital
Philadelphia, Pennsylvania

One

OVER 11 MILLION MEN AND WOMEN IN THIS COUNTRY ARE
divorced; more than 2 million more join their ranks each year (Glick &
Norton, 1976). The divorced can no longer be considered a social minority (the current rate is approximately 40% in the United States), but there
is little consolation for them in these increasing statistics. Those undergoing the divorce process inevitably experience emotional pain and loneliness, and at times, might tend to agree with the Prophet Mohammed that
"divorce is the most detestable of all permitted things" (Epstein, 1974,
p. 19).

Loss of the marital relationship undeniably affects the health of persons. Holmes and Rahe (1967) demonstrated that divorce and marital
separation* rank second and third, respectively, behind the death of a
spouse as events that produce the highest degrees of stress in adults'
lives. Physical illness, accidents, and suicide also afflict the divorced in
significantly higher numbers than the married (Glick, 1976; Gove, 1973).
The rate of hospitalization for mental illness among the divorced is 8–12
times the national average (National Institute of Mental Health, 1974).

Currently, the impact of marital separation on the emotional health of
children from these marriages is receiving much attention in psychiatric
practice and in the literature (Wallerstein & Kelly, 1980). Separating
spouses themselves, however, also at high risk for emotional illness and

---

* In this article the term *marital separation* is used to indicate a process in which the
spouses' separation becomes permanent. In fact, divorce statistics reflect only 50% of the
separations that occur each year; the other 50% end in reconciliations, at least temporarily,
in which the spouses return to live with each other.

breakdowns, have received less than adequate attention in these areas. Consequently, this article will examine the impact of marital separation on the spouses. The unique kind of loss (relationship loss) they experience, their reactions to this loss (the mourning process), and their pathways to recovery (the healing process) are considered. The material has been drawn from the literature on divorce, loss, mourning, and remarriage, as well as the author's clinical and personal experience. Clinical examples are included to guide mental health professionals who are working with spouses undergoing marital separation.

THE MEANING OF LOSS IN MARITAL SEPARATION

Separating partners experience the *loss of a relationship,* rather than that of a person. The lost spouse continues to exist and in many cases to interact with the losing spouse, for example, around legal or financial matters or parenting the children. These continued contacts, however, do not alter the fact that an enormous disruption has occurred in both their lives. Spouses typically report feeling frightened, anxious, and surprised, not having anticipated the effect that leaving their partner would have. These feelings result from the powerful, yet little understood, experience of marital loss.

Marriage has a powerful shaping influence on spouses that they may not consciously appreciate. That some family therapists define it as a third partner in the treatment of the couple suggests that the relationship could be viewed as having a life of its own. Many ex-spouses, indeed, when describing their marriage, indicate a sense that they felt it had gone through its own lifetime—a beginning, high points, low points, as well as an end.

The marital relationship provides a stable, ongoing context in which the spouses can have their most basic emotional needs met. Love, warmth, affection, intellectual stimulation, and sexual desire all may be satisfied here. Moreover, it serves as a primary source of self-definition. The partners develop identities within a sense of who they are and where they fit in the world. When the relationship ends, they may feel confused and fearful, as though they no longer have an identity.

Perhaps the most painful aspect of marital separation is the rupture of attachment bonds that exist between the spouses. These bonds serve as the emotional glue of the marriage. Weiss (1975) likens them to the intense emotional ties that develop between mother and child (Bowlby,

1958) in early life, which carry their fantasized wishes for exclusive and unlimited emotional and physical access to the other. When these bonds are undone, spouses often feel overtaken by a terrible sense of loneliness, a sense that they are no longer at home or secure in their world. This can be so distressing that many marriages in which love has long since vanished and the spouses can barely tolerate each other remain together to avoid these feelings.

Clinical Example #1

Two couples, where one partner in each had been formerly married to the other, came for treatment. The spouses had remarried, but they still lived together in the same house with their new partners. They claimed that they were "still friends." The ex-spouses wanted help to settle some "old arguments" they'd been having since the days when they were married to each other.

The therapist recognized that they had failed to emotionally separate and that the new spouses had been pathologically inducted into the system. Addressing his intervention to the new spouses, the therapist said that he saw no possible solution to these disagreements while they all lived together and that their partners (the ex-spouses) were going to need their help in getting disentangled; otherwise the arguments would continue forever. The new partners were upset by this idea. Gradually, however, their anger at having to put up with the incessant fights and the stress this was causing them began to surface.

In subsequent sessions the former spouses began to realize that they actually had little interest in keeping these fights going, that they were protecting themselves from something else, moving away from each other. The new partners continued to put pressure on them, and the fighting shifted from the old to the new marriages. The therapist reminded them again of his prediction that things would stay tumultuous while they all lived together.

Three months into therapy, both couples decided to move out of the old house into separate dwellings. They began to come to sessions separately as well. Many months of treatment were required to help the new partners understand and work through their prior investments in helping the ex-spouses stay together and the ex-spouses' inability to separate emotionally from their old partners and really commit themselves to their new marriages.

THE MOURNING PROCESS

Separated spouses mourn the loss of their relationship. Mourning, as Freud (1957) described, is, or substitutes for, a natural human response to the loss of an object. It involves a complex set of reactions that are both psychological and biological in nature, that persist over a period of time and that usually involve some diversion or withdrawal of the person's emotional energies from his or her normal life activities. The process must run its own course, not being interfered with or prevented from happening, so that its ultimate purpose can be accomplished: the freeing of the individual to reinvest emotional energies in purposeful activities and new relationships.

In marital separation, the spouses experience reactions that are similar in some ways to general mourning responses, such as those described by Freud (1957), Bowlby (1980), and others. In addition, some of their reactions are uniquely shaped by the realities of the divorce process. The following are typical responses characteristic of mourning during marital separation:

Panic or Distress

Separated spouses report feelings of anxiety, apprehension, the inability to concentrate on work activities or conversations with people, loss of appetite, insomnia, and sudden outbursts of tears and anger (Weiss, 1975). These feelings, generally occurring immediately prior to or following the physical separation, reflect a response to the sudden rupturing (or anticipated rupturing) of marital attachment bonds. The spouses, suddenly faced with the reality of their loss, must adjust. Fortunately, this phase usually lasts only a few days or weeks at most.

Shock

Other spouses report the absence of any feelings at all, again, immediately at the beginning of their separation. This response seems comparable to the numbness that Bowlby reports in spouses who have just learned their spouse has died. The person feels overwhelmed by the reality of the loss and responds with massive denial, temporarily shutting down his or her emotional system.

Anger, Sadness, and Feelings of Regret and Nostalgia

Following these initial responses, partners report low periods, which come and go in cycles and can last for several months. These periods involve feelings of anger, both at themselves and the ex-spouse, at having failed in the marriage, having been left, being in their current situation, and at other things. Sadness often accompanies these feelings, along with the fear that perhaps they have made a mistake, that to separate was wrong. Many find themselves remembering fond moments with the absent partner, satisfying times that they had completely blocked from memory during the last, unsatisfying months of their marriage. These feelings can come in waves, at unexpected moments, and can leave the spouses feeling quite distressed, caught off guard.

Loneliness

Feelings of loneliness also persist for several months. Even though the spouses may be socially active and keep busy with friends, they experience what Weiss refers to as *emotional loneliness,* a sense that they are now alone and isolated in the world. This results from the loss of security of the marital relationship. It is one of the most painful feelings of marital separation.

Scanning

Spouses frequently scan in their memory the events of their marriage to attempt to discover what went wrong, who was to blame, or what their role was in the failure (Krantzler, 1975). This may be a way of preserving the attachment bonds in fantasy. Done in a constructive spirit, this recounting can help the spouses gain valuable insight about their former marriage and help them accept their role and the loss itself. When scanning occurs defensively, so that the spouses avoid the previously mentioned effects, it may prolong the mourning process, even result in depression or other psychiatric symptoms.

Euphoria

A smaller percentage of separated spouses report feeling positive, or high, at the beginning of their separation (Hunt & Hunt, 1977). This is due to a sense of relief, of increased personal freedom, newly gained competence, and a reinvestment of emotional energy, previously tied into the marriage, in themselves. The latter feature explains the fragility of these highs, which, for most, come and go sporadically for several months. Not grounded in solid relationships, these euphoric moods are especially vulnerable to narcissistic setbacks. The spouses often experience plummeting from them to the previously mentioned low periods. These swings in mood do tend to level off, however, within the first year of separation.

Ambiguity and Ambivalence

These are particularly difficult reactions for spouses and are common in the divorce experience. Spouses seem confused as to whether or not they have suffered a genuine loss. The fact that separation was a voluntary decision, undertaken with the hope for a better life, makes it seem less clear-cut as to whether it should be mourned. Similarly, spouses remain confused as to how they feel, or should feel, about the ex-spouse. They may vacillate between feelings of anger and resentment and of tenderness and compassion. Although its intensity usually levels off after several months, ambivalence can persist for years and be rekindled at awkward times when the spouses meet.

These reactions are reinforced by parochial social attitudes that still plague the divorced. No social rituals exist to help guide the spouses through mourning in divorce as they do, for example, when the other spouse dies (Goode, 1964). Likewise, the expectation that separated spouses should be viewed as adversaries intensifies their ambivalence and fails to acknowledge that even in poor marriages, spouses often experience feelings of loss at separation. These social attitudes make the individual's ambivalence reactions more difficult to work through in the mourning process.

Duration of Mourning

This varies widely for partners. Some of them work through many aspects of mourning before they separate. In these cases the marriage loses its viability much earlier, and the partners recognize this consciously. Physical separation, however, adds more stress when it occurs for these cases than for contrasting ones. Most divorce researchers agree that the most painful aspects of mourning peak within the first several months and then level off by the end of the first year (Hunt & Hunt, 1977; Weiss, 1975). Complete emotional resolution occurs when the spouses are no longer significantly influenced by the previously described reactions. This usually takes between 2 and 4 years.

VARIATIONS OF MOURNING EXPERIENCES: NORMAL AND PATHOLOGICAL

Some spouses seem to fare better than others during marital separation. Although none escape without some upset, those who initiated the separation, women, those who have children, and those with custody of their children, all seem to come out slightly better (Hunt & Hunt, 1977). Also, contrary to popular myth, middle-aged people and those who had long-standing marriages do not seem to be more severely affected than younger people or those from marriages of short duration.

Some spouses seem to be severely affected. Those who have evidenced chronic difficulty with separations and who have depressive tendencies may become melancholic and despondent during these times. Their prognosis for recovery from the mourning may be poor unless psychotherapy is initiated. At the opposite extreme are spouses who have severe narcissistic limitations and are able to form only rudimentary attachment bonds with others. They tend to mourn little during separation. Their chances for successful future relationships are also poor without intensive therapeutic work.

Another pathological pattern occurs with spouses who involve their children exploitively in their own mourning processes. Unable to tolerate their own guilt about separating, some parents deny their own painful feelings as well as their children's. They unconsciously withdraw from the children and then focus on their children's responses as problems. In other cases, those who are unable to resolve their anger may triangle their children into ongoing disputes with their ex-spouse. This occurs either through acting out of support or visitation issues, criticizing the other spouse to the child, or criticizing the child for expressing loyalties to the other spouse. In any of these situations, the children end up as scapegoats, and the parents remain immobilized in the mourning process. Family therapy is usually necessary for the entire system to disengage from these rigid patterns of interaction.

Clinical Example #2

A 30-year-old woman, separated for 5 months, brought her 4-year-old daughter for therapy. She complained that since her husband had left, her daughter had been whiny and belligerent. She could not understand her daughter's upset because, as she described, her husband had never been much of a father to the child. In addition, she noticed that the little girl would come up to her at unexpected times and hug her vigorously. She interpreted this as clingy and dependent behavior. Overall, she was worried and perplexed about what to do for her daughter.

The therapist worked with the mother to help her become aware of her own feelings about her separation. The woman was extremely defensive, and, as it turned out, understandably so. At the news of her separation, both her parents harshly reprimanded her, said the breakup was her fault, and refused to talk with her for weeks. She was emotionally shattered and hid her guilt by denying feelings and acting stoic.

The therapist gently urged her to talk about her hurt about the marriage and her parents' reaction. Much anger toward both parties surfaced in the sessions. She began to understand how she had been denying her daughter's pain over losing her father. She was later able to recognize that the daughter's hugs were for her. The girl had recognized her pain and was attempting to console her. This awareness eventually helped her become more responsive and appreciative toward the child. The therapy lasted several months, until the woman was able to acknowledge her own mourning responses in her separation.

RESOLUTION OF THE MOURNING PROCESS

Most separated spouses eventually do recover from the loss of their marriage. Gradually, the pain and confusion resulting from the breakup subside. The partners regain self-confidence, a new sense of identity, and the courage to reinvolve themselves in relationships with the opposite sex. This healing process takes time; however, the spouses can actively initiate steps, at first slowly, then later more vigorously, to speed their recovery.

Garfield (1980) has described various developmental factors that influence the recovery process for separated spouses, awareness of which can facilitate the clinician's work. Three of these factors will be briefly described. A fourth, the transforming of the postseparation relationship between the spouses, will be discussed in more detail.

1. Self-Acceptance

Partners can facilitate their own recovery by openly facing their feelings about the breakup and coming to understand their role in its making.

During the divorce process guilt feelings surface. Spouses often feel bad about themselves and doubt their own capacities to love or maintain stable relationships. Denial of these feelings and displacement of anger and blame onto the spouse only increase the problems. Facing the mourning process with a positive attitude and being willing to reflect on their past behaviors can help the former spouses gain a healthy objectivity about their situation. Their insights can be applied to alter future relationships to prevent repeating destructive patterns.

2. Accepting New Roles and Responsibilities

Marital separation forces spouses to assume new roles and responsibilities. Approaching these with a positive perspective can help the spouses develop a sense of pride in their newly found competences. Men may learn to cook and do their own laundry and ironing, and women may learn to handle finances and home repairs—all things the traditional division of labor may have protected them from doing in marriage.

Some responsibilities may feel burdensome and awkward, such as when women are forced to find employment for the first time in their lives; yet later, these may be viewed as genuine accomplishments. Friedman (1980) points out that, frequently, separated fathers undertaking part-time care arrangements with their children develop better relationships with them than they had when they were full-time fathers.

3. Renegotiating Relationships with Friends and Family

Finding emotional support in friendships and family relationships can greatly benefit separated spouses. The breakup inevitably takes its toll of people who care about the spouses. Both family and friends may be shocked when they hear the news, responding with upset, withdrawal, or in some cases even rejection. In open and honest relationships, however, genuine caring on both sides can transcend the awkwardness and upset feelings. Friendships can deepen as a result, and the separated spouses can achieve a new level of adult-to-adult communication with their parents, whose uncritical acceptance of their separation can greatly help in reducing their feelings of shame. This support also gives the separated person an important sense of affirming the capacity to have other successful relationships in the future.

4. Transforming the Relationship with the Ex-Spouse

Establishing a healthy relationship with each other can be a valuable contribution to the healing process. Most spouses continue to interact after their separation, for example, over legal and financial issues or over their children. Even though these contacts can be awkward, especially at the beginning, they can serve as valuable emotional check-ins, opportunities to see how the other is doing and to measure one's own progress.

One of the most powerful channels for developing renewed trust is through the parenting relationship. Children clearly profit from their parents' cooperation during divorce (Wallerstein & Kelly, 1980); partners also profit from the opportunity to affirm their caring through parenting. Whitaker's (1980) metaphor of children as concrete orgasms or literal representations of the love that exists (or potentially exists) in the marriage applies here. The spouses' continued commitment to their children affirms what was valuable in their past relationship. At the same time, the spouses can also partially rectify the painful situation they have created for their children.

Cooperative parenting after separation not only affirms the best of their former relationship but also facilitates the ex-spouses' emotional separation by providing them with a new model for relating to each other. This replaces the ambivalent, negatively charged model each held of the other as marital partners. Strengthening communication and cooperation around parenting thus can work in a paradoxical way to help the spouses accept the loss of their marriage.

It is naive to imagine that all spouses can achieve this cooperation. For some, the bitterness that has developed between them makes decent communication later impossible. Epstein (1974) and Krantzler (1975) describe the difficulties that most partners have, particularly at the beginning, in trying to remain cordial with each other. Otherwise refined couples report psychoticlike communication in which emotional restraint seems a superhuman task. Nostalgia and separation distress bring others together in desperate but fruitless attempts to reestablish the broken attachment bonds.

Although continued friendship and cooperative parenting may be desirable goals, separated spouses (and clinicians as well) must realize that mutual trust and affirmation develop gradually and in relation to the degree of emotional separation that has been achieved by the partners.

Despite emotional hardships, many spouses are able to work out amicable relationships. Certain guidelines facilitate this goal. During the early phases of separation the spouses must carefully monitor their interactions and attempt to limit contacts to the business at hand (e.g., settling finances, property, custody, and visitation arrangements). If possible, emotionally provocative issues, as well as the often irresistible temptation to attack or further heap blame on the other spouse for the marital failure, should be avoided. The best intentioned spouses, nonetheless, succumb to indiscretions on occasion.

Spouses should also avoid grilling their children about details of the absent spouse's life including their dating habits. Using the children as emissaries of anger and blame or as targets for the spouses' unresolved hostilities is destructive both for children and the partners. Likewise, leaving major decisions about custody or visitation to children who are too young to decide these issues should be avoided.

Clinical Example #3

A 38-year-old divorced woman brought her 14-year-old son to the therapist for behavior problems in school and an uncooperative attitude with her at home. The boy, previously a B student, had fallen dramatically in his grades and become sullen and withdrawn since visiting his father over the summer. The woman spent much of the first session berating her son and comparing his personality to his father's, who she felt was always irresponsible and uncaring during their former marriage. Although the couple had been divorced for 6 years, the mother sounded as though the husband were still in the room. She, herself, was dating and had a steady boyfriend, but could not decide if she would ever marry again.

Subsequent sessions revealed that the boy had become angry about something that had occurred between him, his father, and his new stepmother over the summer. In an individual session he said that he did not want to talk about the incident with his mother because she would say "I told you so," and he would feel even worse.

Raising this in a family session, the therapist pointed out to the mother how angry she was with her son and how she seemed unable to listen to him, as though she were still communicating with her ex-husband through him. He suggested she become more firm with the boy, review his assignments for a while with him, and take more interest in general in him. The mother was able to recognize her projection onto her son and fairly rapidly shift her attitude toward him. He in turn began to perk up, relax his moodiness, and raise his grades at school.

This occurred in the first 3 months of therapy. The woman asked to have individual sessions with the therapist at this point.

She said she felt angry about what had happened in her marriage, was still hurt, and felt this stood in the way not only of her relationship with her son but also with her boyfriend, who now wanted to marry her. Her husband, who had been in business, had gone through a series of failures before he had given up in favor of attending medical school. During their marriage, she had supported him through moody periods, depressions, and even times when he was physically abusive with her and the children. They separated after he graduated medical school. He had left her with bills and two children to support.

Although she understood from her children that her husband was doing extremely well financially, he was always late and sometimes forgot to send his monthly support payments to her. When asked how she responded to this, the woman confessed that she said nothing, just was angry and kept telling herself and the children how typically irresponsible he was acting. In fact she had hardly spoken to him, except superficially, during the last 6 years.

The therapist realized the woman was unconsciously perpetuating certain aspects of her old relationship with her husband, and strongly suggested she take a stand about this issue, to talk with her husband about this. She resisted the suggestion for several weeks, but finally conceded that her passivity was only reinforcing the problem.

She came to a session looking relaxed and pleased with herself. She reported that she had finally gotten the courage to call her ex-husband. He was very embarrassed, apologized for his negligence, and promised to have the money to her on time from now on. More important, however, she said, they were able to share what had been going on in their lives with the children, new relationships, and some genuine regrets and sadness about what had gone on between them. "You know, I think he's really changed, since the marriage," she said. "People really can change over time."

This woman began to change also as the therapy went on. Her ex-husband's support payments began to come regularly, and they talked more frequently about the children by phone. This seemed to have a positive effect on her self-image and her attitude toward her relationship with her boyfriend. Gradually her anger toward men began to subside. She was more philosophical about her divorce and casual about more recent contacts with her ex-husband. She continued treatment for several months until announcing her intention to remarry.

CONCLUSION: IMPLICATIONS FOR REMARRIAGE

Divorced spouses who emotionally resolve their marital losses seem to be better prepared for remarriage (Garfield, 1980; Messinger, 1976; Messinger, Walker, & Freeman, 1978). Eighty percent of divorced spouses remarry within 3 years (Glick & Norton, 1976). Those who have worked through troublesome relationships with former spouses may spare new partners their continuing struggles. If not, the new marriage may inherit endless complaints about (and endless comparisons with) the old one. Battles over support payments and visitation, for example, add to the vulnerability of second marriages, which are already at slightly higher risk (44%) for divorce than first marriages (Glick & Norton, 1976).

Clinicians working with blended families must evaluate the degree to which unresolved mourning blocks progress. The involved spouses must be called on to work through their own feelings of loss and continuing problems with their ex-spouses to avoid burdening the new relationships.

The remarriage itself may be an important resource in the healing process. If the new spouse is sensitive and not threatened by the partner's leftover attachment feelings, he or she can facilitate the separation process by supporting the partner through tough moments with the ex-spouse, helping the partner to accept the complexities of balancing the old relationship with the new one.

There is a need for developing new paradigms for understanding mourning and its resolution in divorce. Bowlby's (1980) widowed spouses suggested that more was involved in resolving their losses than letting go of old attachment bonds. Healthy widows and widowers, for example, reported that they continued to speak and consult with their former spouses in fantasy, years after they had died. These were consoling experiences for them. They had found a way to transform the former relationship to meet their current needs.

This fact suggests that the expectation that former relationships in which spouses were deeply invested can be emotionally erased is not only unreasonable but may be inconsistent with healthy resolution of marital separation. Clinicians may have to help the mourner accept the reality of the old relationship, acknowledge its current role in his or her emotional life, and integrate these in attempts at loving and living in a new family.

REFERENCES

Bowlby, J. The nature of the child's tie to his mother. *International Journal of Psychoanalysis*, 1958, *39*, 350-373.

Bowlby, J. *Attachment and loss* (Vol. 3). New York: Basic Books, 1980.

Epstein, J. *Divorced in America*. New York: Dutton, 1974.

Friedman, H.J. The father's parenting experience in divorce. *American Journal of Psychiatry*, 1980, *137*, 1177-1187.

Freud, S. Mourning and melancholia, 1915, *The complete psychological works of Sigmund Freud*. London: Hogarth Press, 1957.

Garfield, R. The decision to remarry. *Journal of Divorce*, 1980, 4(1), 1-10.

Glick, P.C. *Trends in family formation and dissolution: Implications for policy*. Paper presented at the Groves Conference on Marriage and the Family, March 1976.

Glick, P.C., & Norton, A.J. *Number, timing and duration of marriages and divorce in the U.S., June 1975*. Current Population Reports, Washington, D.C., October 1976.

Goode, W.J. *The family*. Englewood Cliffs, N.J.: Prentice Hall, 1964.

Gove, W.R. Sex, marital status, and mortality. *American Journal of Sociology*, July 1973.

Holmes, T.H., & Rahe, R.H. The Social Readjustment Rating Scale. *Journal of Psychosomatic Research*, 1967, *2*, 213-218.

Hunt, M., & Hunt, B. *The divorce experience*. New York: McGraw-Hill, 1977.

Krantzler, M. *Creative divorce*. New York: Signet, 1975.

Messinger, L. Remarriage between divorced people with children from previous marriages: A proposal for preparation for remarriage. *Journal of Marriage and Family Counseling*, 1976, *2*, 193-200.

Messinger, L., Walker, K.N., & Freeman, S.J.J. Preparation for remarriage following divorce. The use of group techniques. *American Journal of Orthopsychiatry*, 1978, *48*, 263-272.

National Institute of Mental Health, U.S. Department of Health, Education and Welfare. *Marital status, living arrangements and family characteristics of admissions to state and county mental hospitals and outpatient psychiatric clinics, United States 1970* (Statistical Note 100). Rockville, Md.: U.S. Department of Health, Education and Welfare, 1974.

Wallerstein, J.S., & Kelly, J.B. *Surviving the breakup: How children and parents cope with divorce*. New York: Basic Books, 1980.

Weiss, R. *Marital separation*. New York: Basic Books, 1975.

Whitaker, C. Personal communication, 1980.

2. Attachment Loss and Divorce: A Reconsideration of the Concepts

Dorothy S. Huntington, Ph.D.
Center for the Family in Transition
Corte Madera, California

18

Two

ONE OF THE FASCINATING QUESTIONS FOR MENTAL HEALTH
practitioners is, How and why has the relatively simplistic concept of
attachment become so important in the field of custody, divorce, and
remarriage? The growth and maintenance of significant interpersonal relationships, the crux of our humanness, is of crucial importance, yet there
is a tendency to reduce this vitally complex conceptualization to that of
attachment almost as if one were discussing the presence or absence of a
rubber band, a silver cord, or an iron chain.

Yarrow (1979) has suggested that it might be clarifying "to view
attachments from a developmental perspective as part of a chain of cognitive and social developmental changes" (p. 904). Attachment is an
organizing concept that indexes a broad range of behaviors extending
across a wide developmental time span. If attachment is viewed in part as
the formation of, and investment in, significant human relationships, it
can be seen that there are *many* varieties and qualities of these significant
human relationships—some positive, some negative, some anxious, some
evoking sadness, some ambivalent, some happy, some formed on terror,
and some formed on love. What does significant mean in this context?
How does a child draw love; what are the different sorts of love drawn
from different people, and how does the child return love in different
ways, to different people, and at different times? Indeed, is it even
conceivable to lose an attachment?

A RECONSIDERATION OF ATTACHMENT

The capacity to form significant human relationships may be seen in
Winnicott's (1963) terms as the capacity for concern. This capacity arises

as the result of a transaction between a child and a parent who has the ability to give spontaneously the feeling of concern and understanding for the needs of the child. In contrast, some family relationships are formed through hostile accusations between the spouses and self-serving competition as to who is the best parent. The capacity to form significant human relationships grows out of the capacity to feel and the capacity to love, out of the sense of relative stability and order in one's own universe; and ultimately, as development goes on, out of the capacity to introspect, the capacity to be aware of one's own processes, and the capacity to be aware of (and to respect) the needs of others. Attachments are not fully formed at the beginning. Relationships deepen and gain greater meaning as time passes, but the development of the capacity to form such relationships is an early developmental task. The meaning of the child for the parent is crucial to the form this development takes.

Concern, the basis for significant relationships, is a crucial feature of social life and relates directly to an individual's sense of responsibility. An individual cares or minds, and both feels and accepts responsibility. The capacity to be concerned is a matter of health; it is not only a maturational node, but it also depends for its existence on an emotional environment that has been good enough over a period of time. Without reliable parental figures at some point in time, the capacity to develop concern is lost, and its replacement is a primitive form of guilt and anxiety (Winnicott, 1963). The ego capacity to invest in relationships can thus be more crucial in this regard than the content of those relationships.

What are the specific components of parenting skills that seem most significant for the development of this capacity? For the infant in the earliest formation of the capacity to love, the variables that have emerged as most highly related to good development are the sensitivity of the parent in responding to the baby's signals of need and distress and to the baby's social signals; the promptness and appropriateness of that response; the amount of interaction that the parent has with the baby and the amount of pleasure both derive from it; the extent to which interventions and responses are at the baby's timing rather than the adult's; the extent to which the adult is free from preoccupation with other activities, thoughts, anxieties, and griefs so that the adult can attend to and respond fully to the baby; and the extent to which the adult can understand and satisfy the baby's needs, as distinct from the adult's own.

Content of the Significant Relationship

What feelings, what beliefs, and what interchanges are important in each different relationship? Children, capable of relating to them in a variety of ways, respect, understand, and appreciate different qualities in adults. Some adults are quiet and bring peace and thoughtfulness; some are exhilarating and jazzy; some broaden the child's perspective on the world; some help clarify internal feeling states; some create trust; others create distrust, wariness, and fear. Some adults are narcissistically demanding, and yet from others the child learns to expect close attention to his or her own needs. Any of these relationships may be deeply significant. The context of the tie is a crucial factor in the personal perception of the importance of the tie at times of relationship change with the concomitant need for reinvestment in new relationships.

Form and Strength of Relationships

The form of a relationship—anxious binding, mutual dependence, independence, or freedom—in whatever form or context relates to the strength of the bond between persons and the degree of ease or distress involved in the loosening of the bond. It is possible that early, good relationships and a well-developed capacity to form relationships lead to a greater degree of freedom in relating to and accepting new figures. Strength of bonds may involve not just the amount of mutual dependence, but also the ability to replace bonds meaningfully. Weak bonds may be those where people are relatively meaningless in any differential sense, but weak may also refer to relationships that do not allow for replacement. If a person's entire organization is built on one relationship, with the belief that there can never be anyone else, this dependence may be a weakness of basic self-confidence that may have serious consequences. This quality of object tie and its connection to general characteristics of self-image is especially important as we learn more about the degree of anxiety and hate involved, for example, in the extremely strong binding of severely abused children to their abusing parents. On the other hand, a secure sense of trust is not only the basis for significant relationships, but also the main factor that allows for the development of new positive ties and reinvestment in new people after the weakening of old relationships.

Context of Object Ties

The context—not only the number, type, and form of the total series of relationships, but the gestalt of the system of supports within and external to the family is crucial: extended kinship, adequate child care arrangements for working parents, adequate housing and transportation, supportive school programs, adequate medical care, enough money to live on without undue stress, rewarding or at least minimally satisfying jobs, and helpful friends. What happens on the day-to-day level in the context of the family has a far more important impact on attachment than has been previously recognized.

The importance and complexity of the form of early and continued relationships with siblings, friends, grandparents as well as parents, neighbors, teachers, ministers, caregivers in and out of the home, and so on, are now recognized. These relationships are seen as increasingly important contexts for primary parent–child relationships as well as crucial in their own right. Very important also are the second-order effects: for example, the way one parent treats a child is a function of what the other parent is or is not doing with the first parent. The presence or absence of an ex-spouse or the quality of the enduring bonds, positive and negative, between parents long after divorce have a major impact on the type and quality of relationship between a parent and a child.

If our society is heading away from the direction of the traditional nuclear family, then our understanding of children's larger social networks is extremely important. For example, "Although it was long believed that preschoolers were not socially capable of having real friends, children as young as three years form distinctive friendships that are surprisingly similar to adults' friendships and love relationships. Some preschoolers have relationships that are strikingly reminiscent of the attachment of adult spouses, with a camaraderie of adult co-workers, or even between those of adult mentors and their protégés" (Collins, 1981). Children's early extended, nonfamilial relationships are much stronger elements in character formation than has hitherto been believed. The impact of changing American family styles on children's development is also crucial in conceptualizing attachment bonds. Although social development theorists traditionally viewed the mother–infant relationship as primary, its exclusivity and uniqueness have long been challenged. Frank Pedersen (cited in Collins, 1981) has said: "Going beyond that relationship, mapping out a wider array of influences and relationships, is based on an appreciation of the greater cognitive competence of the infant and its ability to enter into multiple relationships. In recent years the picture has changed dramatically. To mothers, we have now added fathers, siblings, peers, uncles, aunts, you name it." Michael Lewis (cited in Collins, 1981) has said in a similar vein that there is a large network of potentially important figures affecting any child's development. Lewis' social network model can account for the way that children may satisfy their needs by turning to a mother, a father, a sibling, or a peer. Ultimately, Lewis has said, it all comes down to one word—love. "In social science, we don't use the word love, so we find acceptable substitutes—like the word 'attachment.' But we're talking about love here, pure and simple. You can love many people in many ways, and finding love is a process that goes on throughout one's life."

ATTACHMENT AS A DEVELOPMENTAL CONCEPT

The formation of the ability to care, to be concerned, and to give and receive love depends on the transactional relationship of what a child brings to the world and what happens in that world, to child-rearing practices, parental expectations and characteristics, societal characteristics, and institutional demands and expectations. Of crucial importance in the development of dysfunctions are child-rearing practices with inconsistent patterns of care; lack of predictable sequences of response; presence of frequently shifting figures; rapid alternation from extreme violence and abuse to loving, kissing, and affection, and to being left completely alone; and lack of regularity resulting in an inability to predict from one moment to the next what will happen. One thinks here of the concept of habituation, an important feature of the usual parent–child relationship. The ability of the parent and the child to predict each other's actions is essential because it imposes environmental regularities that are extremely important in the development of internal, early regulatory mechanisms that are the basis of ego formation and object ties. These regularities are missing in disorganized families.

What is good and what is bad are arbitrary in a disorganized family system, depending on the personal whim of the adult or an older sibling, rather than being a shared value. Since this is so, predictability is low. One does not learn to take a certain action because that action will have a certain reward; one learns to relate solely to the adult or older sibling and to guess in advance what is wanted or tolerated at any moment.

Of extreme importance in this type of interaction is the fact that rules are not information-giving devices, but rather punitive measures, so that cognitive processes are not to be used creatively, but for the avoidance of danger. In Robert White's terms, this type of cognitive and personality organization would represent fighting the rear guard actions rather than advancing (White, 1963).

Our traditional concepts of the basic nature of intrapsychic, social, and intellectual functioning are open to question when the child's ego must precociously take over the protective function that should be the responsibility of the environment. When this happens in the early preverbal stage, action and not language becomes the medium of communication and defense. This type of action does not contain the roots of mastery, but only of avoidance of positive human relationships. Children learn early to read cues in the environment for manipulating people. Pavenstedt's (1967) description of the children as 3-year-old con men in *The Drifters* is masterful. If action language continues beyond its appropriate developmental stage, a basic defect in the ability to form symbols is present, which is then reflected in defects in abstracting and defects in processes of thought that are basic to the understanding of human relationships (as well as to academic skill acquisition). The children are action oriented by virtue of their style of cognitive capacity.

The defect in abstracting may lead equally to a distorted ability to understand complexities and thus to a distorted sense of reality of human life. Action rather than thought may become the basis for coping with the world, and there may be a defective ability to think about, and thus recognize, the needs of other people. The ability to symbolize (to form abstract concepts) is seen as basic to the development of a cognitive grasp of the world, one that recognizes the importance both of other people and of intellectual content.

A child's growing sense of competence and effectiveness in dealing with the world is built from many sources starting with earliest infantile experiences—an expectation of gratification of most needs, most of the time; an ability to predict the consequences of actions with a reasonable degree of certainty; and the corollary, of being able to produce an effect on the animate or inanimate world, to have someone care.

> The feeling of being able to have some effect on people, to get them to listen, provide some of the things we need, do some of the things we want, receive some of the love and help we want to give—this feeling of social competence is a substantial foundation stone of self-respect and security (White, 1963).

The presence of this self-respect and security in the family prior to divorce shapes in a crucial way the fate of the object ties after divorce.

Importance of Adults in the Life of a Child

Adults serve as figures for identification in learning how to cope, how to handle feelings, how to approach and solve problems, how to think and explore, how to deal with others, and how to respect, accept, and value differences and similarities in other children and adults.

Adults serve as people who care about the child, who show the child that the balance of rewards is greater than disappointment, who show the child that the child is someone special, and who show the child that by and large the world is an interesting and even exciting place to be, as someone the child can trust.

Adults serve as figures who radiate a sense that the child can learn and love and is expected to learn and love in the broadest sense. Enthusiasm and expectations are infectious. If parents assume that reinvestment in new people is possible and desirable, children will have a far easier time in making this reinvestment, but there is no one-to-one correlation, for indeed children are not just reflections of their parents. The child's own individual sense of loyalty and self is of major importance, as indeed are individual differences in every facet of personality.

Individual Differences

The importance of individual differences among children has been largely ignored in the writings concerning attachment bonds. It has been assumed that all children are equally capable of forming similar attachments. Little attention has been paid to individual differences in characteristics that may modify capacity as well as content, form, and strength. Nonetheless, this is a crucial area for future study, since the freedom to form new relationships or to give up old ties may be an essential issue in postdivorce planning in terms of custody and visitation, as well as for considerations in remarriage. The tempo and temperament of a child— whether the easy child, the difficult child, or the child who is slow to warm up (Thomas & Chess, 1977)—responsiveness, sensitivity, adequacy of controls, the ease of making transitions from one situation to the next, the coping style, and the number and types of significant relationships a child tolerates or thrives on are all more important than has been previously discussed. Only with specific attention to these individual differences will mental health practitioners be able to fully assist children and families of divorce and remarriage.

Also of great differential significance is the role of motivation to reach out to others versus motivation to hide and defend one's self. A positive self-image, reasonable self-confidence, relative independence, self-esteem, freedom to try new activities, and a sense of competence and trust all lead in a different direction in terms of the maintenance of important human relationships. In contrast a sense of helplessness, failure avoidance, apathy, anxiety, depression as an ego state, and a basic expectation that the world is a miserable place to be (chronically, not just at a particular moment in time) do not enable individuals to maintain relationships. In essence, attachment has been seen only as an interpersonal and emotional bonding, but we must at this time look at it in a broader sense of cognitive and structural strengths as well.

FAMILY TIES

The need for a more complex model of human development leads also to a more careful, more sophisticated analysis of the role of the family in the development and maintenance of a child's attachment bonds.

The report of the Carnegie Council on Children noted:

American social science habitually has studied the psychological, social, and intellectual development of children in relative isolation from the social context in which they live. Parents have been studied in much the same way. Although social scientists, politicians, and social theorists often pay lip service to the role of underlying social forces in children's lives, we have found little systematic study of these factors. Experts, lay people, parents, and children themselves, seldom think concretely about the impact on children's lives of such things as the jobs parents have and the unemployment rate. . . . Until policy makers and planners shift their focus to the broad ecological pressures on children and their parents, our public policies will be unable to do much more than help individuals repair damage that the environment is constantly reinflicting. Abandoning the tendency to deal with children in isolation from their families or the society they live in is a prerequisite for policies that will clearly support families and children (Keniston, 1977).

CONCEPTUALIZING THE IMPACT OF DIVORCE

Escalona (1975) has said that conventional psychological theory seems insuffic' nt to account for societal influences on child development. Much of current psychological theory is inapplicable to the effects of shifting or absent parental figures or of violence and brutality in society upon its younger members. Much of what has been written about attachment needs to be rethought. The deteriorating or strengthening of relationships over time is a crucial issue in the family after divorce.

Hess and Camara (1979) have discussed divorce as a potentially disruptive factor in the normal progress of a child's development on the basis of the threat to primary bonds, the creation of loyalty conflicts that may require developmentally inappropriate levels of sensitivity and thought, and the disruption of internalized conceptions of social reality. The child needs to reorder internal representations of familiar external patterns. Concepts of roles of mother and father and perceptions of the permanence of relationships must be revised. "Divorce is a cognitive puzzle for the child, bringing dissonance and inconsistency to the child's social and affective world. To deal with loss and to rearrange the disrupted perceptions demand time and energy that must be withdrawn from the work of the schoolroom and from social interaction with peers" (Hess & Camara, 1979, p. 82). Family relationships that emerge after divorce, after the dust settles as it were, may affect children as much or more than the divorce itself. It is the postdivorce family adjustment and circumstances that serve as mediating factors in the vicissitudes of attachment bonds.

What then are some of the factors that the transactional model of child development leads us to consider in thinking about attachments, divorce, and remarriage?

1. For the child
   - the child's cognitive and emotional assimilation and understanding of the divorce and the subsequent remarriage
   - personality traits, flexibility, temperament, tolerance for stress, handling of effects, adaptive behaviors, and areas of competence
   - developmental level and prior developmental tasks accomplished
   - the sex of the child and siblings

2. For the parent
   - each parent's emotional health or relative narcissistic injury

- the effects of being a single parent: in terms of the economy; on discipline and order; emotionally; and practically, in terms of child care arrangements and the like
- the remaining bonds with the ex-spouse; the desire to continue the battle or to resolve it
- remarriage and the quality of that new relationship. The dynamics are very different for the cases where both parents remain single, where either custodial or noncustodial parent remarries, or where both remarry.

3. For the parent–child relationship
  - quality of total family interrelationships, prior to and after divorce
  - parental needs for the child for emotional support
  - loyalty conflicts
  - custody and visitation battles and agreements
  - the effects of parental absence directly on the child and indirectly via the impact on the remaining parent

4. For the context
  - the life event changes that coincide with divorce
  - outside supports and support networks—social groups, extended family, and so on.
  - economic realities
  - prior and current levels of discord—conflict prior to and after divorce
  - the changes over time. Divorce does not set people in concrete; the outcome is not predetermined.

SUMMARY

"Our society allows adults to have multiple marriages but children are reared to love and trust only their natural parents" (Thies, 1977, p. 59). Perhaps this is the key to the discussion of changes in attachment. Can children really be raised now in such a way that allows for multiple attachments? Margaret Mead (cited in Thies, 1977, p. 60) has said that "each American child learns, early and in terror, that his whole security depends on that single set of parents." What if, indeed, we now consider the reality of children of divorce and remarriage who may be raised by many caregivers, children who need to relate to a large number of people and to have attachments and loyalties of many kinds to many different people. Are these the children of the future? Ultimately, children must achieve workable solutions to maintaining significant human relationships to many different people. Perhaps, in a reconsideration of the concept of attachment we as mental health practitioners will find new ways to help children in finding their solutions.

REFERENCES

Collins, G. A new view of childhood. *This World*, March 1, 1981.

Escalona, S. Children in a warring world. *American Journal of Orthopsychiatry*, 1975, *45*, 765-772.

Hess, R., & Camara, K.A. Post-divorce family relationships as mediating factors in the consequences of divorce for children. *Journal of Social Issues*, 1979, *35*(4), 79-96.

Keniston, K., and Carnegie Council on Children. *All our children: The American family under pressure.* New York: Harcourt Brace Jovanovich, 1977.

Pavenstedt, E. *The drifters.* Boston: Little-Brown, 1967.

Thies, J.M. Beyond divorce: The impact of remarriage on children. *Journal of Clinical Child Psychology*, 1977, Summer, *6*, 59-61.

Thomas, A., & Chess, S. *Temperament and development.* New York: Brunner/Mazel, 1977.

White, R. *Ego and reality in psychoanalytic theory.* Psychological Issues Monograph. New York: International Universities Press, 1963.

Winnicott, D.W. The development of the capacity for concern (1963). In *The maturational processes and the facilitating environment.* New York: International Universities Press, 1965.

Yarrow, L.J. Historical perspectives and future directions in infant development. In J. Osofsky (ed.), *Handbook of infant development.* New York: Wiley-Interscience, 1979.

3. The Relationship between Former Spouses: A Fundamental Subsystem in the Remarriage Family*

*Work on this article was supported by NIMH Project No. 1 Rol MH 34397-01 Al "Postdivorce Relationships: The Binuclear Family." The first author is principal investigator.

31

Constance R. Ahrons, Ph.D.
School of Social Work
University of Wisconsin-Madison
Wisconsin Family Studies Institute
Madison, Wisconsin

Morton S. Perlmutter, Ph.D.
School of Social Work
University of Wisconsin-Madison
Wisconsin Family Studies Institute
Madison, Wisconsin

Three

RISING DIVORCE RATES INDICATE RADICAL SHIFTS IN traditional American values and life styles associated with marriage and family. A projection from current trends indicates that 40% of the American children in the next decade will spend some of their childhood years in a divorced family arrangement (Bane, 1976); 80% of these divorced families will eventually become remarriage families (Norton & Glick, 1976). Given these current remarriage rates, it is estimated that about one fourth of all children growing up today will have more than two sets of parents before they reach the age of 18 (Furstenberg, 1979).

The child of divorced parents who both remarry will have two biological parents, two stepparents, and a range of possible combinations of biological siblings, step- and half-siblings, up to eight grandparents (even more if any grandparents had divorced and remarried), and any number of extended relatives through the new spouses of the biological parents. Family therapists with an orientation that dictates working with the whole family system will find themselves faced with a huge network when counseling a remarried family. Compounding the complexities of this large and complex remarried system is the lack of a consistent model of divorce therapy on which a model of postdivorce family therapy including remarriage can be built.

The scarcity of research and theory development of divorced family processes results in part from the fact that the postdivorce family has no historical precedent in western society. Theoretical approaches focusing on the family have generally not incorporated divorce and remarriage into their developmental frameworks. In light of heated courtroom debates and new custody arrangements such as joint custody, it is also surprising that research on the relationship between former spouses who collaborate as parents is very limited (Ahrons, 1981c). Equally surprising is that although remarriage has received recent attention from both researchers and clinicians (Duberman, 1975; Messinger, 1976; Walker, Rogers, & Messinger, 1977), the delicate and complex relationship between parents and stepparents (i.e., between the mother and the stepmother) has not been studied.

POSTDIVORCE FAMILY RELATIONSHIPS

Single-Parent Family: A Misnomer

Divorce is usually thought to be symptomatic of family instability and synonymous with family dissolution. This view is reflected in the terms used to describe the divorced family, such as *broken home, disorganized, fractured, incomplete, single-parent family,* and so forth. This view has given rise to a distorted perception of divorce, leading investigators and practitioners to focus primarily on pathology. It has also led to a genre of research focused on father absence and hence has excluded the relationships between fathers and mothers and fathers and children. The term *single-parent family* implies that a family contains only one parent; however, in many divorced families, both parents continue to function in parental roles. Divorce creates new households with single parents, but it results in a single-parent family only when one of the parents, usually the father, has no further contact with the family and does not continue to perform a parental function. More appropriate terminology would distinguish between these two circumstances and would describe the former as a one-parent household.

Although the loss of the father–child relationship is an inevitable outcome for many children in divorced families, innovative custody arrangements and the increased involvement of fathers in child-rearing roles have also created postdivorce family arrangements in which the children continue to be reared by both parents. In such cases, divorce has not terminated family relationships; rather, it has been a process whereby the form of these relationships has changed.

A more realistic framework for clinical intervention with divorced families requires a model that does not regard divorce as pathological. Such a model would recognize various options for reorganizing the postdivorce family and would incorporate criteria for evaluating the relative strengths and weaknesses of such options.

The Binuclear Family: A Redefinition

When divorce is viewed as a process that results in family reorganization rather than disintegration, a different picture of divorced families emerges.

Based on a family systems framework, Ahrons (1980a) has conceptualized the divorce process as a normative process of family transition and change. Identified are five major family transitions spanning the process of emotional divorce through family reorganization and redefinition. The latter two transitions incorporate remarriage as an integrated part of the divorced family's reorganization.

The divorce process can be viewed as a series of transitions that mark the family's change from nuclearity to binuclearity. The reorganization of the nuclear family through divorce frequently results in the establishment of two households, maternal and paternal. When both spouses remarry, these two households become maternal and paternal stepfamily subsystems. These two interrelated households (or nuclei of the child's family of orientation), however, form one family system—a binuclear family system (Ahrons, 1979, 1980c). Among postdivorce families, the importance of each of the households varies. Some families make distinct divisions between the child's primary and secondary home (i.e., sole custody), whereas in other families both homes have equal importance, (i.e., joint custody). The relationships between the two households in the binuclear family vary also. For many families, special events and holidays stimulate a desire for the two households to join. Some binuclear families regularly share holidays and birthdays; others have biweekly or monthly get-togethers serving as family meetings or conferences for problem solving. Still others choose not to join the two households under any circumstances. Hence, the term *binuclear family* indicates a family system with two households, whether or not the households have equal importance in the child's life experience.

Relationships between family members in the binuclear system are determined by the type of relationship established between the biological parents (the former spouses). This gets even more complicated when both parents remarry and the binuclear family then becomes composed of two stepfamily households (Ahrons, 1981b). Although binuclear families share some similarities with extended kin networks, the lack of socialized norms to guide the binuclear family's functioning results in undefined and ambiguous role expectations.

Former Spouse Relationship

Except for the few references in the literature to an amicable divorce (Ahrons, 1979; Blood & Blood, 1979; Framo, 1978), contact between divorced spouses is usually perceived as an indication of unresolved marital issues and hanging on to the marriage (Kressel & Deutsch, 1977). It is interesting to note that although the general public, clergy, and mental health professionals decry the divorce rate and its familial implications, we nevertheless continue to view postdivorce ex-spousal bonding as pathological or quasi-pathological. In a recent study that explored the views of lawyers, clergy, and psychotherapists toward divorce, Kressel and his colleagues (1978) found that

> With a few notable exceptions, there was a general distrust of the ex-spouses' continuing involvement with each other as friends, business partners, or lovers, largely on the grounds that such attachments reflect separation distress rather than realistic caring, and they drain emotional and physical energies that would more productively be spent in forming new relationships. (p. 138)

The general mistrust of a continuing relationship after divorce is reflected in the prevailing stereotype that former spouses must, of necessity, be antagonists; otherwise, why would they divorce? This stereotype is again reinforced by a bias in the available clinical material. Clinicians tend to see only the difficult or problematic former spousal relationships; well-functioning divorced families are less apt to seek professional intervention. Because the literature on divorce is primarily clinical, role models of successfully divorced families have been lacking.

Just as the relationship between married spouses is a critical determinant of family interaction, so too is the relationship between divorced spouses critical to divorced family reorganization and interaction. One of the most stressful tasks facing divorcing parents is that of redefining their coparental relationship—the relationship between both parents that permits them to continue their child-rearing obligations and responsibilities after divorce. The process of coparental definition requires that divorced spouses separate their spousal and parental roles, terminating the former while redefining the latter. This difficult and somewhat paradoxical process forms the nucleus of divorced family reorganization and redefinition (Ahrons, 1980c).

Although a continued, cooperative, and mutually supportive relationship between divorced parents has been noted to reduce the crisis-potentiating stress associated with divorce (Hetherington, 1979; Wallerstein & Kelly, 1980), its dynamics remain relatively unexplored. Recent research on the effects of divorce on children indicates that the relationship of the noncustodial father both to the former spouse and to the child are critical factors affecting the child's adjustment. Continued involvement of the father, characterized by free or open access between father and child, coupled with a mutually supportive and cooperative coparental relationship, were found to result in better psychological adjustment of the child (Hetherington, Cox, & Cox, 1976; Wallerstein & Kelly, 1980). Research combining these two factors suggests that a continued relationship with the father is dependent in part on the relationship between the divorced parents (Ahrons, 1979, 1981c).

The Coparental Relationship

Findings from the Binuclear Family Research Project, a longitudinal investigation of 98 divorced families, indicates that there is much wider variation in the way former spouses relate than the current literature suggests (Ahrons, 1981a). The majority of the former spouses (85%) reported a continuing relationship with one another 1 year postdivorce (approximately 2 years after separation). The relational styles were varied and formed a continuum that ranged from "my former spouse as best friend" to "my former spouse as bitter enemy." Most of the respondents clustered around a broad midpoint in the continuum, which can best be described as "neither friend nor foe." About 65% of the mother-custody sample and 85% of the joint-custody couples reported having conversations either in person or on the phone at least once a month; about one third of both groups reported weekly interactions.

For most of the respondents in this group, interactions were child focused; however, about one fourth of the mother-custody and half of the joint-custody couples reported frequent interaction as well about issues unrelated to their children. Of this group of parents who continued to relate with each other as former spouses, about 20% of the joint-custody but only 5% of the mother-custody couples described their relationship as intimate. In only two couples did this intimacy include occasional sexual relations. Another 30% of the joint-custody and 20% of the mother-custody couples were less intimate, but they reported relationships and feelings for each other that were generally caring, respectful, and friendly. For this group, the content of their interactions centered around their extended families and mutual friends. Intimacies, such as dating or discussions about the reasons for the divorce, were rarely, if ever, shared by the vast majority of the couples.

At the bitter enemy pole of the continuum were about one third of the mother-custody and one fifth of the joint-custody samples. Some of these couples reported interacting rarely, resorting to the use of a mediating third party such as a lawyer or counselor to settle family issues. Others in this group reported frequent interactions that were always angry or hostile.

To assess whether the relationship between former spouses was important to these parents in and of itself, rather than persisting solely because of the children, all respondents were asked if they still would want to relate to one another if there were no children. Over one third of the mother-custody and over half of the joint-custody samples said that they would.

These findings suggest that the desire to maintain a relationship with one's former spouse may be prevalent among the divorcing population. Further investigation of actual relationships between former spouses is needed to provide a better understanding of what can be considered normal or pathological in the relationships of former spouses. Caring feelings and friendly interactions appear to be normative and should not be dismissed automatically as an indicator of unhealthy or destructive attachment between former spouses. Many of the couples interviewed had relationships that were predominantly "kin" or "quasi-kin" in nature, based on the couples' shared history, including extended family and friendships formed during the marriage. Given that the average length of marriage in the sample was about 10 years, it does not seem too surprising that these former spouses continued to share some of the less conflictual, and perhaps still rewarding, aspects of their past lives together.

Family Reorganization and Redefinition

The redefinition of relationships in the binuclear family depends on the relationship between the biological parents. The growing debate about custody rights reveals the lack of knowledge about the time-honored concept, "the best interests of the child," and brings the custom of sole custody into serious question. A trend toward shared custody and coparenting seems to be emerging ("One Child, Two Homes," 1979), which should have profound implications for the postdivorce family. Underlying the custody controversy is the basic question of whether divorced parents can cooperate well enough to share custody without harming the child's emotional development. Proponents of joint custody, such as Roman and Haddad (1978), argue that divorced parents can and should share custody. However, sole-custody proponents, such as Goldstein, Freud, and Solnit (1973), argue that divorced parents cannot cooperate sufficiently well to provide the continuity of care necessary to the child's emotional well-being. Given current societal changes such as increased role sharing and equality in marriage, the increase of women in the labor force, and increased parental involvement of fathers, the issue is no longer whether divorced parents can continue to share parenting effectively, but how they can do so.

How the divorced family redefines itself, both to itself and to community and friends, is critical to the family's struggles with identity, boundaries, and individuation. The continuance of meaningful attachments between parents and children is dependent on the kind of relationship that develops between the parents (Ahrons, in press) and between stepparents and parents in the binuclear family system. Rules defining when and how each parent continues to relate to the children are critical to the child's understanding of the divorce and remarriage and to the consequent stabilization of parent–child relationships. Each parent and stepparent must establish an independent relationship with the child, but the continuation of each parent–child unit requires the continued interdependence of the former spouses and stepparents. The concept of family boundaries, the rules that determine the parameters of the family system (Minuchin, 1974), helps to explain the major stresses associated with this transition. The absence of clear boundaries creates much of the confusion and distress. Once the family has established some basic ground rules for separate living units, the parents need to clarify rules for relating within and across the various elements within the family subsystem. The relationship between the former spouses is the foundation for how the divorced and remarried families will redefine themselves; this relationship also determines the emotional climate in which this redefinition will occur (Ahrons, 1980b).

THERAPEUTIC GUIDELINES FOR THE BINUCLEAR FAMILY

We have laid the groundwork in the foregoing section for the centrality of the former-spouse relationship in the remarriage relationship. The research clearly indicates that when there are minor children, a mutually supportive and cooperative relationship between former spouses is in the best interests of the children in the divorced family. However, no research is currently available that assesses how this continuing relationship between former spouses affects new family formations after divorce. There is some speculation, however, that remarriage creates a new crisis in the divorced family that may result in temporary disequilibrium in the family. In most developmental theoretic frameworks of the family, the addition of a new family member such as a baby or adult child returning home to live is assumed to require a period of transition; for some families this results in a major crisis; in other families, though, the transition is relatively smooth. It follows, then, that the addition of a new family member (stepparent) to the binuclear system has the potential to create a crisis within that original relational system. A period of transition is necessary as the new family member identifies the roles he or she will play and understands the rules of the existing family system. Given the lack of clear norms and role expectations for stepparents, however, the transition for most divorced families is usually a difficult and confusing one.

Therapeutic Assumptions

Our work with binuclear families is based on several assumptions. First, we accept the findings of the research and clinical literature and assume that a continuing relationship between former spouses is necessary if they are to successfully coparent their minor children. The term *coparenting* is used here to describe the relationship of divorced parents who both continue to enact their parenting roles and responsibilities. The degree of parental role responsibility and custody arrangements can vary. Second, we assume that the divorced or binuclear family consists of the original or biological family members and any new relationships that are formed postdivorce, either through cohabitation or remarriage. This includes both primary (i.e., children) and extended kin (i.e., grandparents) of the new partner. Third, we assume that the new partnership needs to be simultaneously independent of and interdependent with the members of the earlier partnerships.

From these assumptions we are in the process of developing strategies aimed at helping divorced and remarried families create a binuclear family structure that is functional to both the old (the former spouses) and new elements (new marital partners). Within this general orientation, all family relationships need to be examined in terms of subsystem functioning. Again, as with all other aspects of binuclear family relationships, there is a larger, more complex network to understand than in the nuclear system. Major subsystems of the binuclear family with two stepfamily households are (a) the new partnership (remarriage partners), (b) the old partnership (former spouses), (c) the biological parent and stepparent of the same sex (i.e., mother and stepmother),* (d) each parent and child, (e) each stepparent and child, and (f) sibling subsystems (i.e., biological siblings and biological stepsiblings).

Educational Objective and Family Structure

We concur with the conclusions drawn by Messinger (1976) that remarried families are in need of education to assist them in constructively reorganizing their family. Hence, we feel responsible to inform the families we counsel of current research and clinical knowledge that appear helpful to them in their reorganizational process. A first step when we see the family is to explore with them how they have reorganized their family from the time of divorce through the one-parent household phase into the new remarriage transition. We then ask them to assist us in diagramming their binuclear family so that we can visualize the structure; we use the family diagram to explore relationships among and between subsystems.

---

*We find ourselves encumbered in our writing by the lack of language for describing these relationships. Except for two recently developed terms, *binuclear* and *coparent*, the language describes relationships in postdivorce families only in terms of the past rather than present tense (i.e., former spouse or ex-spouse). Ahrons (1980c) has diagrammed these relationships in the binuclear family and has identified those relationships for which no adequate descriptors exist. This deficit in our language denotes the lack of institutionalization of these relationships, and hence the lack of norms or rules to govern them.

We then label the family as binuclear and address them that way throughout our sessions with them. This serves as a means of reframing their view of their family. We see the education of the family about constructive ways to restructure their family unit as one major aspect of our role as family therapists.

The lack of a systemic model of the divorce process has led to confusion and conflict for many families when they reorganize postdivorce. The "single-parent misnomer" has resulted in role models for divorced family redefinition, leading to the exclusion of the noncustodial father. Research conducted on other family crises, such as missing-in-action families, indicates that it is functional for family adaptation to "close out" and exclude the absent member (father) from the family (Boss, 1977). Even though this has not been explicitly identified in the literature as a final stage in the divorce process, ample evidence exists which suggests that this coping strategy has been common both to divorced families and to our thinking about them. Recent research, however, has revealed that this pattern of coping with postdivorce family reorganization results in increased individual stress and family dysfunction. The more the noncustodial father is closed out of the system, the more dysfunctional stress the system experiences. Noncustodial fathers with infrequent postdivorce contact with their children were reported to be more depressed (Greif, 1979), more dissatisfied with their relationships with their children (Ahrons, 1979), and more stressed regarding role loss (Keshet & Rosenthal, 1978; Mendes, 1976). Sole-custody mothers were more depressed and overburdened by the responsibilities resulting from role overload (Brandwein, Brown, & Fox, 1974; Hetherington et al., 1976; Weiss, 1980). Children with limited or no father contact suffered the most severe developmental and emotional distress (Hetherington, 1979; Wallerstein & Kelly, 1980).

Many remarriage units are clearly resistant to viewing themselves as part of a binuclear family because they do not want to include the former spouse as part of their family. We differ only in semantics from Walker and Messinger (1979), who note that "it may be useful to conceptualize the remarriage family as consisting of persons who have dual memberships in two families" (p. 191). The conceptualization of the binuclear family assumes two households or subsystems of the family with persons having dual membership across the two. Walker and Messinger (1979) also note that "these two 'families' would have to learn to live with two sets of relatively permeable boundaries, rather than the relatively imper-meable ones of the nuclear family household" (p. 192). This major difference between nuclear and binuclear families is one that most remar-riage units have difficulty accepting at first because it appears to threaten their existence in the only structure they know, a nuclear family. The importance of helping the remarried unit to accept the importance of permeable boundaries can often be a first step to their being able to build up a tolerance for living with the ambiguity it brings as well as to be able to set relationship rules and clarify roles within the system.

Interdependence and Intimacy

An important part of our work with binuclear families is to facilitate their acceptance of the need for continued interdependency between the former spouses. The remarriage unit needs to develop rules for the role that the former spouse will continue to play in their current life. They need to understand that the former spouse has parental rights and respon-sibilities and that to enact these usually requires some continuing relation-ship between the former spouses. The nature of that relationship is deter-mined by the history of their relationship prior to the remarriage and how that relationship is perceived and received by the new partner. We try to help the former spouses to articulate and define what kind of relationship is possible and to determine whether the relationship is detrimental to the new binuclear family and how the old relationship can be maintained separate from the new relationship. Our focus is always on the task of parenting and what relationships are required to enact those roles. Al-though there are a wide range of possible stepfamily configurations (Visher & Visher, 1979), we focus on the basic subsystem relationships.

This aspect of our therapy is aimed at helping the families consciously design their family style. A major determinant of family style is based on the level of intimacy that is desired or can be tolerated among the adults in the system (Perlmutter & Hatfield, 1980). We have worked with families in which the mother and stepmother have shared the major aspects of child rearing and have cooperated effectively with one another. However, we have also worked with other systems in which the mother and stepmother have been threatened by the relationship that the mother has with the father, or the mother has been threatened by the stepmother's relationship with the child; in these cases we have helped the families work out specific rules for their interactions and have helped them delineate the parental roles each will play. The relationship between the mother and stepmother is a delicate one—we tend to see more mother and stepmother pairs than father and stepfather pairs because men tend to remarry sooner and in greater numbers than women—which has the potential to have great impact on the functioning of the binuclear system.

Structuring Sessions

We should note here some of our operational principles guiding the selection of family members who are present in the sessions. Our referrals are varied. Sometimes a child is referred because of behavior problems and the remarriage issue is not presented as primary; sometimes the remarriage unit presents itself as the ''identified patient''; sometimes the family or some of its members are referred by the court for an issue concerning visitation or custody. In all cases we attempt to bring the entire binuclear family unit in for the first session. Most frequently we meet with considerable resistance to this format and have to talk with and support several family members by phone prior to scheduling the first appointment. They often need to be reassured that we will exercise control over the situation and that we will not permit chaos to occur. We comfort them with the understanding that it may be difficult for all to have face-to-face contact and sit in one room; we assure them that we will be in charge and will separate them if and when it seems indicated. We always try to have our first session inclusive of all members and then make decisions after that session for whom we will continue to see, in which dyads or subunits. Future decisions are based on that first session when we assess whether the entire unit will be able to let their defenses down in the presence of the total family group or whether we need to see specific subsystems to deal with some of the issues in the family. We may then decide to see each stepfamily unit (with or without children), then perhaps see the biological parent subsystem separately and occasionally see the same-sex biological parent and stepparent subsystem (i.e., mother and stepmother). Depending on the age of the children and the identified problems in the system, we may also see parent–child subsystems separately. Whenever possible we try to have a closing session with the whole binuclear system in which we assess the changes and decisions made by the family.

Our decisions for which subsystem to see are flexible and are determined by the level of intimacy that the family seems able to tolerate, the nature of the relationships, and the types of personalities involved. We also weigh the issue of the strength of the remarriage unit, since open confrontation within the former spousal subsystem in the presence of the remarriage unit may only serve to weaken that remarriage unit.

At this time we are unable to state with any degree of certainty which style works best. We are continuing to experiment with different groupings; perhaps in time we will be able to state more explicit guidelines for structuring sessions, but we tend to think that binuclear family structures are too complicated and have too many configurations to establish hard and fast rules.

REFERENCES

Ahrons, C.R. The binuclear family: Two households, one family. *Alternative Lifestyles,* 1979, *2,* 499–515.

Ahrons, C.R. Divorce: A crisis of family transition and change. *Family Relations,* 1980, *29,* 533–540. (a)

Ahrons, C.R. Joint custody arrangements in the postdivorce family. *Journal of Divorce,* 1980, *3,* 189–205. (b)

Ahrons, C.R. Redefining the divorced family: A conceptual framework for postdivorce family system reorganization. *Social Work,* 1980, *25,* 437–441. (c)

Ahrons, C.R. The binuclear family: An emerging lifestyle for postdivorce families. *XIXth International CFR Seminar on Divorce and Remarriage,* Leuven, Belgium, August 30 – September 4, 1981. (a)

Ahrons, C.R. The binuclear family: Two stepfamilies, two houses. *Stepfamily Bulletin,* 1981, *1*(2), 5–6. (b)

Ahrons, C.R. The continuing coparental relationship between divorced spouses. *American Journal of Orthopsychiatry,* 1981, *5,* 415–428. (c)

Ahrons, C.R. Predictors of paternal involvement postdivorce: Mothers' and fathers' perceptions. *Journal of Divorce,* in press.

Bane, M. Marital disruption and the lives of children. *Journal of Social Issues,* 1976, *32* (1), 103–117.

Blood, R., & Blood, M. Amicable divorce: A new lifestyle. *Alternative Lifestyles,* 1979, *2,* 483–498.

Boss, P. A clarification of the concept of psychological father presence in families experiencing ambiguity of boundary. *Journal of Marriage and the Family,* 1977, *39,* 141–151.

Brandwein, R.A., Brown, C.A., & Fox, E.M. Women and children last: The social situation of divorced mothers and their families. *Journal of Marriage and the Family,* 1974, *36,* 498–514.

Duberman, L. *The reconstituted family: A study of remarried couples and their children.* Chicago: Nelson-Hall, 1975.

Framo, J. The friendly divorce. *Psychology Today,* February 1978, pp. 76–79; 100–102.

Furstenberg, F. *Remarriage and intergenerational relations.* Paper presented at the Assembly of Behavioral and Social Sciences, National Academy of Sciences, Annapolis, Maryland, March 22–24, 1979.

Goldstein, J., Freud, A., & Solnit, A.J. *Beyond the best interests of the child.* New York: Free Press, 1973.

Greif, J.B. Fathers, children and joint custody. *American Journal of Orthopsychiatry,* 1979, *49,* 311–319.

Hetherington, E.M. Divorce: A child's perspective. *American Psychologist,* 1979, *34,* 851–858.

Hetherington, E.M., Cox, M., & Cox, R. Divorced fathers. *The Family Coordinator,* 1976, *25,* 417–428.

Keshet, H.F., & Rosenthal, K.M. Fathering after marital separation. *Social Work,* 1978, *23,* 11–18.

Kressel, K., & Deutsch, M. Divorce therapy: An in-depth survey of therapists' views. *Family Process,* 1977, *16,* 413–443.

Kressel, K., Lopez-Morillas, M., Weinglass, J., & Deutch, M. Professional intervention in divorce: A summary of the views of lawyers, psychotherapists and clergy. *Journal of Divorce,* Winter 1978, *2,* 138.

Mendes, H. Single fatherhood. *Social Work,* 1976, *21,* 308–312.

Messinger, L. Remarriage between divorced people with children from previous marriages: A proposal for preparation for remarriage. *Journal of Marriage and Family Counseling,* 1976, *2,* 193–199.

Minuchin, S. *Families and family therapy.* Cambridge, Mass.: Harvard University Press, 1974.

Norton, A.J., & Glick, P.C. Marital instability, past, present and future. *Journal of Social Issues,* 1976, *32*(1), 5–20.

One child, two homes, *Time,* January 29, 1979, p. 61.

Perlmutter, M.S., & Hatfield, E. Intimacy, intentional metacommunication and second order change. *American Journal of Family Therapy,* Spring, 1980, 17–24.

Roman, M., & Haddad, W. *The disposable parent.* New York: Holt, Rinehart & Winston, 1978.

Visher, E.B., & Visher, J.S. *Stepfamilies: A guide to working with stepparents and step-children.* New York: Brunner/Mazel, 1979.

Walker, K.N., & Messinger, L. Remarriage after divorce: Dissolution and reconstruction of family boundaries. *Family Process,* 1979, *18,* 185–192.

Walker, K.N., Rogers, J., & Messinger, L. Remarriage after divorce: A review. *Social Casework,* 1977, *58,* 276–285.

Wallerstein, J.S., & Kelly, J.B. *Surviving the breakup: How children and parents cope with divorce.* New York: Basic Books, 1980.

Weiss, R.S. *Going it alone.* New York: Basic Books, 1979.

4. The Father-Child Relationship Subsequent to Divorce

Judith Brown Greif, D.S.W.
Division of Child and Adolescent Psychiatry
Albert Einstein College of Medicine
New York, New York

Four

DIVORCE IS ONE STAGE IN THE LIFE CYCLE OF A FAMILY. THE resolution of a divorce, particularly in regard to issues such as custody and visitation, critically affects the restructuring of the family. It determines how the individual members will continue to relate to one another and, therefore, has implications for the family not only at the point of divorce but throughout future stages such as remarriage.

Significantly, social policy about divorce still does not adequately reflect social change within the family. One of the major tasks confronting separated and divorced families is the preservation of meaningful parenting of the children. Yet, in the overwhelming majority of cases, divorce still results in sole maternal custody of children and a profound dilution of the father–child relationship. This cultural bias toward maternal custody stems from the notion that mothers are and should be home full time with their children, and that fathers neither want nor need to be more than peripherally involved. Such assumptions discount the profound sex role changes that have emerged in the past decade, resulting in the moving of women in greater numbers into the labor force and the reintegrating of men into family life, and ignore the increasing body of knowledge about the importance of fathers to the healthy growth and development of children. Surprisingly, at a time in our society when men are becoming more involved with their children during marriage, they are still being disposed of as parents when the marriage dissolves. Such restructuring of family functioning during a divorce has significant implications for every member of the family.

FATHERING

Until recently the definition and value attached to fathering in American society had little to do with a man's direct interaction with his children. To be a good father meant being a good provider. Caring for the children was women's work. Recent developments have altered these roles and assumptions. Advanced industrialization has reduced work hours, providing increased time for men to be available to their families. In addition, the Women's Movement, with its emphasis on greater equality in the labor force as well as at home, has radically accelerated a change in sex roles and produced a new consciousness in parenting. Concurrent with increased numbers of women choosing to leave home and find work, men are being urged to enhance their parenting skills and reintegrate into family life (Levine, 1976). However, the high degree of involvement that a father may have with his children during a marriage may be seen as inappropriate or become impossible when the marriage dissolves (Green, 1976). Custody of children is still overwhelmingly awarded to the mother at the time of divorce, and the father–child relationship is then governed to a large extent by limited visitation periods.

It is symptomatic of the low value our society places on the father–child bond that until recent years there has been such a dearth of studies on fathering. Parenting has been equated with mothering; researchers examining parenting styles and experiences have even relied on mothers to supply the thoughts and feelings of fathers.

Paradoxically, we first grew to understand the impact of fathering by its absence rather than by its presence. There is a vast body of research on the effects of paternal deprivation on children (Biller, 1974; Lynne, 1974). Those studies reveal that children who grow up deprived of a father suffer significant difficulty in a number of areas of development— sex role identification, academic achievement, cognition, and moral development. Despite the considerable research on father absence, it is only in recent years that we have begun to question, let alone examine, the impact of child absence on fathers.

IMPACT OF DIVORCE

The literature and research that first emerged on divorced families tended to center on that part of the family that remained together (i.e., the mother and children) and often ignored the father. More recently, research has emerged that explores the impact of divorce on the entire family (Hetherington, Cox, & Cox, 1976; Roman & Haddad, 1978; Wallerstein & Kelly, 1980a). Gradually a picture has emerged of the specific issues inherent in the relationship between children and fathers after divorce. Some of these issues are examined in the sections that follow.

Loss

One of the critical issues for fathers and children in the traditional postdivorce family is an overwhelming sense of loss. The structure imposed via restricted access and decision making has severe repercussions on the father–child bond. In sole custodial arrangements, the child's limited access to a noncustodial father is often interpreted as abandonment and may result in the child's depression, lowered self-esteem, or behavioral symptomatology (Wallerstein & Kelly, 1980b). There is also significant mourning by the child for the absent parent that can become all-consuming, leaving the child little energy to devote to other pursuits such as play, academic studies, and the establishment and enjoyment of other relationships.

Parallel with the child's mourning, fathers with limited access to their children continually complain of feeling shut out of their children's lives (Greif, 1979; Hetherington et al., 1976). Hetherington et al. (1976) note that "a pervasive concern of the fathers was the sense of loss of their children. For most this declined with time, but for many it was a continuing concern" (pp. 426–427). Many fathers seem to cope with this loss, as well as their feeling of being devalued as a parent, by limiting their involvement with their children. Visitations between noncustodial fathers and children become not joyous occasions, but enormously painful reminders of all they have lost. Many fathers, unable to tolerate the pain and overwhelmed by their persistent attachment to children they cannot see, eventually drop out.

Parents who are deprived of custody, are significantly limited in the amount of time they may spend with their children, and are legally restricted from major decision making and responsibility vis-à-vis their child often stop seeing themselves as parents. As reported elsewhere (Greif, 1979), the less time a father spends with a child, the less he sees himself as a parent and the less he is then motivated to continue to be involved in the child's future growth and development.

Conversely, fathers who are able to maintain meaningful time and responsibilities with their children continue to feel reinforced and satisfied in their role as parents and are less likely to withdraw from their children (Greif, 1979; Keshet & Rosenthal, 1978). In fact, such fathers often grow and thrive in their parental role subsequent to divorce, specifically through having the opportunity for time to parent, rather than just visit with, their children. For example, Keshet and Rosenthal (1978), in their study of fathers who shared parenting of their children after divorce, found that men who assume significant child care responsibilities "find that the demands of that responsibility can become an important focus for their own growth" (p. 18), resulting in the father's new-found sense not only of himself but also of his children.

With few exceptions, research indicates that the crisis of divorce can be lessened for every member of the family when children are able to maintain open and meaningful access to both parents (Roman & Haddad, 1978). The continuation of substantial time between the child and each parent preserves the relationships after divorce and thereby protects the family system from the stress of dealing with additional loss.

Superficiality of Relationships

Fathers and children with limited mutual access after divorce continually feel the need to court one another, to indulge the other to ensure that the visits will not end. Fathers become sugar daddies, buying presents and entertaining the children. Children are afraid to address unpleasant issues, particularly anger at the noncustodial father, for fear he may not want to return for another visit. It is easy for a child to express anger at a parent who will be there the next morning, but it is frightening when it is a parent the child may not see again for a long time.

Limited visitation is continually overshadowed by the impending good-bye. No sooner do the father and child feel comfortable with one another than it is time to separate again. To protect themselves from such vulnerability, noncustodial fathers and children, often unknowingly, maintain relationships on a superficial basis, afraid to open up and discuss feelings because of the rapidly approaching pain of another good-bye. This emotional distancing interferes with a father's ability to attend to the emotional needs of his child and therefore reinforces the disintegration of his perception of himself as an adequate parent.

This sense of superficiality has not been found to be a significant issue in father–child relationships when the fathers have continued to coparent the children after divorce. As reported elsewhere (Greif, 1979), fathers who were able to maintain substantial contact with their children after divorce "described relationships with open expression of a whole range of emotions. They did not feel as shut out from their children's inner life, and sensed that their continuous availability to the child over time allowed for the child's more spontaneous sharing of feelings" (p. 315).

Time Alone with One's Child

Visitation is traditionally granted regardless of the number of children in the family. If a father has one child or five, that factor rarely affects the amount of time he is allotted with his children after divorce. One of the serious problems faced by noncustodial fathers and children is the preservation of necessary time alone on a one-to-one basis. Fathers with more than one child, who are restricted in access to their children, often feel conflict about seeing one child at a time because of the long period until they can see the others again. They miss the intimacy of time alone, yet cannot tolerate the guilt and pain associated with choosing to see one child and not the others.

REMARRIAGE

Remarriage represents a further attempt by the family to reorganize. As such, it may reactivate conflicts and issues thought to have been resolved at the prior stage of divorce.

Loss is a major issue for fathers and children subsequent to divorce and can re-emerge significantly at the point of remarriage. A remarriage can jeopardize the access between parent and child. It often represents an additional loss for a child who fears abandonment by the remarried parent. When the parent who remarries is a noncustodial father with limited access to his child, the threatened loss is exacerbated by the prior experience of divorce, which resulted in increased distance between father and child. When the custodial parent remarries, the child's mourning for the absent noncustodial parent may interfere with the child's capacity to form a meaningful relationship with a new stepparent.

Although there is a common assumption that diminishing a child's relationship with a biological parent promotes the development of a relationship with the same-sexed stepparent, research and clinical experience demonstrate the reverse. Children often feel as though an unequal distribution of their time with each parent is reflective of their having been made to choose the stepparent over the absent biological parent. As has been reported (Messinger, Walker, & Freeman, 1978): "If children can continue the relationship with the absent parent without being expected to choose sides, they will not feel abandoned and this, in turn, will leave them freer to accept the reality of the marital breach and to feel clearer about the role of their parent's new spouse" (p. 270).

Given these stresses, it is noteworthy how little attention has been paid to the impact on remarriage of alternative forms of custody that diminish the notion of an absent parent. It may be that the experience of providing a child with continual and substantial time with both parents following divorce may in fact blunt the experience of loss at the stage of remarriage. One could hypothesize that a coparenting arrangement might also ease the potential for a child s conflicting loyalties. By maintaining open and meaningful access to both parents, the child is not made to feel as though he or she has chosen one parent over the other.

Another issue central to the step family is the stress associated with having to accept the child's membership in two households. It is suggested by the results of some studies that the factor of a child's attachment to a parent living elsewhere creates a variety of problems: competition between same-sexed adults, difficulty in sharing children, and problems in controlling the child (Visher & Visher, 1978; Walker & Messinger, 1979). Noncustodial fathers whose ex-wives remarry feel even more threatened in their parental role because of the reality that the new stepfather has greater access to, and therefore perhaps greater influence on, his child. Custody arrangements that foster the bonding of both parents to their child after divorce may protect a parent from feeling like an absent disposed parent and therefore may diminish the threat posed by the entry of a same-sexed stepparent into the family system.

In summary, just as the strains of divorce derive in great part from the disruption of the father–child bond, so too the stress of remarriage may be exacerbated by the child's inaccessibility to both parents. It would appear that shared parenting after divorce, which allows for sufficient time between the child and both biological parents, may protect the entire family system at the point of remarriage by decreasing the experience of loss, by blunting the potential for conflicting loyalties on the part of the child, and by mitigating competition between the adults (Greif, 1980).

INTERVENTION

Families in the process of separation, divorce, and remarriage may require help in understanding the issues and stress related to the particular stage in the life cycle of their family. As discussed previously, one of the most significant issues concerns the feelings of attachment and loss between a noncustodial father and his child. Professionals who work with these families can provide help in a number of ways.

1. Families at the point of divorce need to be educated about the particular stresses of divorce as they impact on different members. A mother needs to be advised about the significant pressures and anxieties of being a single parent and should be encouraged to arrange for sufficient child-free time to pursue all the different aspects of her new role, not only as a parent, but also as a woman who may want to socialize, continue her education, obtain a job, further a career, and so on. A father needs to be advised about the importance of remaining actively involved as a parent so as to avoid feelings of depression, role loss, and alienation between himself and his child. Parents need to be educated about the impact of divorce on children, in particular the trauma of a child being denied meaningful access to both parents.
2. Both parents need to be educated about alternatives to traditional sole-custody arrangements and about different possibilities for continuing to share parenting of their children. As Roman and Haddad (1978) have noted: "In crucial ways, what people think about themselves and believe to be their options are the most formidable barriers of all" (p. 150). Parents need to be helped to consider which custodial arrangements best protect and encourage the attachment between a child and both parents, not only at the point of divorce but through the remarriage stage as well.
3. Families need assistance in establishing a working relationship vis-à-vis their children. One priority is to help them separate the remaining marital conflicts from parental issues. Professionals can also be helpful in aiding families to rework custody arrangements that are no longer functional.

After separation and divorce, families may require intervention in some or all of the following areas:

1. Fathers deprived of custody may require considerable support to stay actively involved with their children, as parents emotionally and physically, rather than to withdraw. Groups for fathers may be

particularly helpful in addressing those issues. Similarly, sole custodial mothers may require encouragement in fostering, rather than thwarting, a child's relationship to a visiting father.

2. Children and visiting fathers may need help in gaining confidence expressing feelings with one another, particularly anger directed at each other. Fathers may need assistance in reassuring children that limited access need not be synonymous with a lack of caring.

3. Fathers may need practical education about child care. Professionals can help noncustodial fathers plan meaningful time with their children, despite the change in structure and environment, to preserve the continuity of the relationship.

CONCLUSIONS

Divorce traditionally creates a structure with inherent conflict: the significant removal of a father from the life of a child. The issues of attachment and loss between a noncustodial father and child are very real, and the resulting problems reverberate throughout the entire family system. Yet, it appears that alternative forms of custody that provide both mother and father the opportunity to continue meaningful parenting of their child protect the family by preserving the father–child bond throughout the strains of the divorcing process. Such coparenting may blunt some of the stress of remarriage as well.

REFERENCES

Biller, H.B. *Paternal deprivation.* Lexington, Mass.: Lexington Books, 1974.

Green, M. *Fathering.* New York: McGraw-Hill, 1976.

Greif, J.B. Fathers, children, and joint custody. *American Journal of Orthopsychiatry,* 1979, *49,* 311–319.

Greif, J.B. *Remarriage and joint custody.* Paper presented at the annual meeting of the American Orthopsychiatry Association, Toronto, April 1980.

Hetherington, E.M., Cox, M., & Cox, R. Divorced fathers. *The Family Coordinator,* October, 1976, 417–427.

Keshet, H.F., & Rosenthal, K.M. Fathering after marital separation. *Social Work,* 1978, *23*(2), 11–18.

Levine, J. *Who will raise the children? New options for fathers (and) mothers.* Philadelphia: Lippincott, 1976.

Lynne, D.B. *The father: His role in child development.* Belmont, Calif.: Wadsworth, 1974.

Messinger, L., Walker, K., & Freeman, S. Preparation for remarriage following divorce: The use of group techniques. *American Journal of Orthopsychiatry,* 1978, *48*(2), 263–272.

Roman, M., & Haddad, W. *The disposable parent.* New York: Holt, Rinehart, & Winston, 1978.

Visher, E., & Visher, J. Common problems of stepparents and their spouses. *American Journal of Orthopsychiatry,* 1978, *48,* 252–262.

Walker, K., & Messinger L. Remarriage after divorce: Dissolution and reconstruction of family boundaries. *Family Process,* June, 1979, 185–192.

Wallerstein, J.S., & Kelly, J.B. *Surviving the breakup: How children and parents cope with divorce.* New York: Basic Books, 1980. (a)

Wallerstein, J.S., & Kelly, J.B. Effects of divorce on the visiting father–child relationship. *American Journal of Psychiatry,* December 1980, 1534–1539. (b)

5. A Developmental Approach to the Treatment of Children of Divorcing Parents

Bonnie Robson, M.D.
C.M. Hincks Treatment Centre
Toronto, Ontario, Canada

Five

IT IS ESTIMATED THAT BY 1990, 33% OF OUR NATION'S children will experience their parents' divorce before they reach the age of 18 (Glick, 1979). Some children appear highly resistant and cope well with the crisis of divorce. Others may show initial symptomatology lasting from 1 to 2 years, followed by a return to a normal developmental pattern. Some unfortunate children develop severe psychopathological reactions. Factors that differentiate these groups include the personality of the child, the child's age at the time of the divorce, the sex of the child, the amount of hostility generated in the family prior to and following the divorce, the relationship with siblings, and the availability and capacity for significant adult contact to assist the child with adaptation (Anthony, 1974; McDermott, 1968; Rutter, 1971).

For both clinical and nonclinical samples, the developmental stage of the child at the time of the divorce or separation has been related to both the quantity and quality of the children's reactions. Preventative intervention, assessment of needs, and treatment focus for severe symptoms should be oriented to the developmental phase of the child. Kurdek (1981), studying the reactions of children ages 8 to 17, noted developmental differences and suggested that they are related to the cognitive developmental stage of the child rather than the specific age.

INFANTS AND PRESCHOOL CHILDREN

It is during infancy and the preschool years that children rely most heavily on their parents. The parents are the child's natural environment and thus help to form his or her perception of the world. Thus, any change in parenting behavior or in interaction with the infant will be reflected in the infant's conduct and developmental progression. Developmental tasks during these years can be described under cognitive, psychological, and psychosocial (Table 1). Cognitively, by 6 months of age, infants are able to distinguish objects in their environment and are starting to differentiate self from others. This begins the process of development of object permanence that occurs during the second year of life. Once object permanence is established, infants are able to make predictions about the behavior of those adults in their environment and, when separated from them, hold a memory map of where they might be. Between 3 and 5 years of age, the child manipulates objects that become named entities and progresses to symbolic play. The child is able through play to recapitulate and gain understanding of situations or incidents that are frightening or distressing.

Psychologically, the healthy infant makes an active attempt to establish a relationship with a responsive caregiver. During the first 6–9 months, the infant develops an attachment to his or her primary caregivers. When the parents provide responsive care or *good enough mothering,* to use Winnicott's (1953) term, the child develops a secure base or trust of the environment and is able to move out into exploration of the world. At 18 months of age, children are at the height of attachment to their parents and show marked behavioral changes if their parents leave them, even for brief periods. Children who have been exploring this new environment perceive the world as having some pitfalls and appear in need of refueling before beginning a true separation–individuation phase, which starts about the third year of life. At this time children begin to assert their own sense of self by opposing the will of their parents. Children experience anger at conceding their own wishes to obey their parents and fear punishment from them. This fear is often denied and turned into a fear of imaginary dangers or monsters.

Psychosocially, by 2 months of age, infants respond differently to their mothers, fathers, and strangers (Als, Tronick, & Brazelton, 1979). By 9 months of age, infants "make strange," seeking the protection of their parents when meeting new people or entering an unfamiliar environment. A young infant can use a blanket or special toy to substitute for this security in the absence of the parent. A transitional object or security blanket appears to operate as a magical protector from harm. By 3 years of age, the developing child wants to play with peers, is interested in the

Table 1 Developmental Phase–Specific Treatment of Children of Separated Parents

| Phase | DEVELOPMENTAL TASK | | | PREVENTIVE MEASURES | | |
	Cognitive	Psychological	Psychosocial	Needs	Symptoms	Treatment
Infancy (years 0–3)	• 6 mo. begins distinguish self/other • 12 mo. development intentional behavior • 12 mos. to 24 mos. object permanence	• 6 mo. makes strange • 8–9 mos. attachment • 18 mos. height of attachment • 15–18 mos. to 2½ yrs. • 16–18 mo. retains object constancy on self	• 2 mo. differential behavior to mother, father, stranger • 9 mo. makes strange, smiles for familiar faces • transitional object	• responsive, good enough parenting • consistent, predictable routines • 1–2 primary caretakers	• feeding problems • toileting problems • regressive behavior • disturbed sleep patterns	• parent counseling
Preschool (years 3–5)	• true symbolic play	• establishes sense of self by opposing will of parents • anger at giving up own rules to obedience to parents • fear of punishment	• interest in peers • interest in difference between boys and girls • imitates behavior of same-sex parent	• needs to be told what's happening • needs security routines and discipline consistently maintained	• frightened, confused, clinging, whiny, needy • regression to earlier behavior patterns • anxiety • negative behavior patterns • highly resistant to change	• parent counseling • individual play therapy • individual psychotherapy for parent

Table 1   continued

Phase	DEVELOPMENTAL TASK			PREVENTIVE MEASURES		
	Cognitive	Psychological	Psychosocial	Needs	Symptoms	Treatment
Early school age (years 6–8)	• forms concepts • forms rules based on grouping of objects	• magical thinking • defenses of denial and pretending	• mastery of skills • plays active games by rules • stable friendships	• allow expression of feelings • frequent regular visiting, easy access • clear custody decision • help with guilt feelings • consistent discipline	• pervasive sadness, crying, suffering, experience loss • fearful nightmares • guilt • wants reconciliation	• individual play therapy
Older school age (years 9–12)	• moral understands, states, changes • judgment and intelligence appropriately used	• knows self as a person • feelings of self-worth • danger, pain avoided	• home centered • plays games with elaborate rules	• talk with neutral adult • honesty, avoid blaming game • insist on visiting • maintain close contact with nonresident parent	• shock and surprise • intense anger • blaming and rejecting one parent • dependency conflicts	• group therapy • family therapy

Adolescence (years 13–18)					
early	• formal operations • abstract reasoning	• regression "I want, I need"	• changes friends	• some separateness from family worries • noncompetitive parent	• shock, not surprise • pain, loss of family • anger at loss • pseudomaturity • acting out, delinquency, promiscuity	• peer group counseling
mid		• autonomy, "I don't need anybody"	• peer-centered crushes	• needs parent not friend • needs discipline		
late	• adult moral development	• intimacy, "I want to be understood"	• adult whole-person relationships	• needs to talk with neutral adult and peers		

difference between boys and girls, and begins the process of imitation, which eventually results in identification with the same-sex parent.

In a separation or divorce, infants and preschool children do not seem to react initially to a parent's leaving home any more than they would to a normal daily separation. This lack of reaction is dependent on the child's degree of secure attachment. Separation, physical illness, or change in the environment heightens the attachment behavior of young children. They become more clinging and use a primitive defense of denial to deal with unpleasantness.

After the initial phase, young children may experience intense separation anxiety. There are two possible explanations for the intensity of this reaction. These children understand, albeit primitively, that their parents no longer love each other and are no longer living together. They feel that if this can happen to their parents, they too can be abandoned. An alternate explanation is that having lost one parent, they have already experienced abandonment. Fearing that they will be abandoned by their other parent as well, they regress to more childish behavior, recalling that when they were babies they were loved and cared for and were in close proximity with their parents. Symptoms of soiling, smearing, enuresis, and struggles with feeding appear. Parents who are already under stress frequently become angered, instead of providing additional love and security. Although opinions vary, many authors feel that younger children react most strongly to separation. Hetherington, Cox, and Cox (1979) state that preschoolers react most to separation. Early responses of anger, fear, depression, and guilt are common. For preschoolers, cognitive development is insufficient to enable them to interpret the events correctly. However, this does not mean that they should be denied an explanation. Children in this age group repeatedly state that they miss the nonresident parent. Such statements may anger the custodial parent; however, he or she should be helped to appreciate that this expression of loss does not mean that the child loves the resident parent any less. If possible, the parent should be encouraged to allow the child to express anxiety regarding the loss and the wish to see the nonresident parent.

Follow-up studies seem to indicate that preschool boys living with their mothers are less well adjusted than girls (Hetherington et al., 1979; Santrock & Warshak, 1979). Very young children, however, appear to be able to attach to substitute caregivers and are more accepting of a new marital partner as a psychological parent than any other group.

Treatment

In planning a primary preventative approach for preschool children, the education and involvement of the parent is of primary importance. Parents must understand the child's need for increased love and security. Parents must be aware and be helped with the problem that their children may regress. Even though the parents may have insight into this regression, they should nonetheless maintain consistent discipline. They must understand that discipline in itself offers security.

In the case of remarriage, the nonresident parent may require additional emotional support and understanding. The parent will frequently witness the child's developing an attachment to the stepparent. A father with whom the author consulted was attempting to travel 1,300 miles by car each weekend to be with his 2-year-old son. He had no place to take his son other than to a motel room. During these visits, he was trying to explain to his son that he was the boy's real daddy. Despite his efforts, the father was shattered by the experience of his son running to his stepfather with open arms calling "Daddy, Daddy." The father had to be assisted to relinquish his own wishes and desires in favor of supporting his son's integration into the reconstituted family. This example should not be construed as a recommendation that biological parents relinquish their rights in favor of stepparents in all cases. Many teenagers express the need 10–15 years later for reassurance that their biological noncustodial parent made every attempt to maintain contact with them during these early years. Teenagers express hurt and anger that their parent failed to fight to see them and suffer resulting disturbances in self-esteem and self-image.

Young children who show severe anxiety symptoms, negative behavior patterns, temper tantrums at the suggestion of change, frequent crying, or frightening nightmares may require treatment intervention. Parent counseling, focused on providing schedules and discipline and increased love and security, is still the treatment of choice for this age group. Wallerstein and Kelly (1975) note that preschool children tend to deny their sadness; however, it appears, through fantasy. On their own they are unable to obtain relief or mastery of the impact of their parents' divorce through play and require the special expertise of therapeutic involvement.

Filial therapy can be particularly helpful in those instances in which a child has not become securely attached to the resident parent and is clinging and demanding toward the nonresident parent. In such instances, a triangulated family pattern often appears with the nonresident parent acting as Santa Claus and encouraging the disturbed interaction between the resident parent and the child. Filial therapy involves working together in play therapy with both the custodial parent and the child to improve their relationship. Adequate parenting skills and the development of compliance behavior on the part of the child are encouraged.

YOUNG SCHOOL-AGE CHILDREN

Children from 6 to 9 years of age rush into their new world. They begin to cognitively form rules based on groupings of objects. They understand that cars, trucks, and airplanes belong to the grouping of transportation and that tables and chairs are furniture. In these primitive concrete groupings, they begin to develop explanations for the world; however, psychologically, these children during their early school years still tend to use primitive defenses to protect themselves against anxiety. They use denial and have a sense of magical thinking. Many children in this age group are oriented toward their peers and toward movement, running, climbing, and playing actively. They are able to walk independently to school and to cross the road safely. They can use the telephone and form stable relationships with their peers. Since these children are oriented toward movement, they tend to show their stress through disruptive behavior, being hard to control and disobedient.

Young school-age children appear the most vulnerable. Children 5–6 years old seem anxious, aggressive, and moody and frequently have temper tantrums (Kelly & Wallerstein, 1976). The children have an intense sense of the family as a unit. They experience separation as an immediate loss of the family, even if family life has been unpleasant and full of tension. Children of 7 or 8 are sad and tearful and sometimes have trouble getting to sleep or have nightmares. Billy, age 7, lives with his mother in the city approximately 500 miles away from where his father lives. Billy suffered from nightmares, fear of the dark, and fear of monsters. He wished to have his mother all to himself, a normal Oedipal wish. When this happened in reality, he feared retribution from his father. His fear of monsters was his primitive way of expressing this conflict. With parental counseling and a few play therapy sessions, all of his symptoms disappeared.

Like preschool children, young school-age children frequently feel responsible for the separation and experience a great deal of guilt. This sense of guilt appears to result because children would rather believe that they did something that caused the marriage to dissolve, which permits the hope that if they are good, their parents will get back together. Then the idealized parent can be retained—the child sees himself or herself as bad and is saved the painful thought that the parents rejected him or her. School refusal, unexplained illnesses, truancy, and behavior problems are not uncommon. Some children will attempt anything to get their parents back together. Parents who are concerned about their child's sudden change in behavior may indeed get together to discuss what should be done. This reinforces the behavior and confirms for the child that his or her actions can bring the parents together—hence, the negative behavior may escalate. Two years later, even despite remarriage, children of 7 or 8 will still be hopeful that their parents will reunite.

No matter how frequently the child visits the nonresident parent, it never seems enough. Jon, an 8-year-old boy, was enchanted with being with his father during his summer vacation. He said that he did not want to return to the east coast to his mother. In an assessment interview, it became apparent that the boy, truly torn between his parents, could not bear leaving one to go to the other.

After 4 years, these children view divorce in a very negative way. Jacobson (1978) reports that the greater the interparent hostility, the greater the maladjustment of the child.

Treatment

Parents of young school-age children must realize how important it is for them to meet together despite their animosity. If possible, they should work out a plan together before presenting it to the children, particularly regarding custody and access issues. When initially explaining to the children about the separation, they should meet with the children together. They must be aware of the children's natural feelings of guilt even if these are not openly expressed. Reasons for the separation should be given to these children to help them appreciate the difference between ongoing parental love and a marital union. The nonresident parent should be encouraged to have frequent visits and to allow the child to telephone whenever he or she wants. It can be most anxiety reducing if the child has easy access to both parents, even during business hours. The parents should be aware that failure to continue regular visiting may result in the withdrawal of the child's affections.

Throughout all developmental phases it is important to educate the parents in maintaining consistent discipline and to avoid overindulging the child. When a child presents severe behavioral symptomatology, individual play therapy may be indicated. The goals of play therapy are to assist with mastery of the situation through play and through the use of creative imagination. Important steps are reaffirmation and acceptance of rules as well as the development of tolerance of change and the development of new rules. In 1976, Wilkinson and Bleck reported that 20% of the children enrolled in elementary school in their school district had parents who divorced. In Florida the figure for kindergarten and first-grade classes was at the 40%–50% level. The introduction of children's divorce groups led by elementary school counselors with specific strategy to meet the needs of children of divorce was found to be extremely successful. Such groups should focus on the developmental model of counseling and include play activities and crafts.

OLDER SCHOOL-AGE CHILDREN (9–11 YEARS)

Shock and surprise are the first reactions of older school-age children to the initial separation. Incredulity and disbelief are healthy defensive mechanisms. Children in this age group still employ denial to a great extent. In the phase of development just prior to the upheaval of adolescence, all parts of their lives are controlled. These children enjoy schedules and planned activities, are rigid about rules, and will argue endlessly before starting a game in order to establish the rules and regulations. They hold strongly to the principle of fair play. Rules are based on the strong identification with parental guidelines. Cognitively, children at this age begin to understand concepts of change in object state in preparation for formal operations and abstract thinking during adolescence. The child psychologically knows himself or herself as a person, has a sense of self-worth, is capable of avoiding danger and pain, and socially plays complicated games with elaborate rules.

When parents separate, the myth of an ideal parent is destroyed. A child in this developmental phase can become intensely angry, usually at the nonresident parent. Kelly and Wallerstein (1976) report that these children appear poised and sober but are evidently struggling for mastery of their emotions, and that they are consciously angry. Once their initial anger decreases, they may assume that their parents are still angry with each other; thus, they are vulnerable to the propaganda game. They will accept, without question, bitter or false statements by one parent about the other.

These children experience loyalty conflicts but fail to express them openly and may resolve the conflict by excessive overdependence on one parent and complete rejection of the other. Susan, who is 11 years old, is unable to go out without her mother. She does not play with friends after school, preferring her mother's company. When the mother and daughter were interviewed, they sat huddled together on a couch. It was difficult at first to pry them apart, even getting them to sit in separate chairs. Susan's mother had to be encouraged to reassure Susan that she felt comfortable in Susan's absence, that she expected Susan to do things on her own.

Sometimes children hang on for years to the image of one parent as all good and one parent as all bad. They frequently become enmeshed at their own volition in the custody struggle. This is a dangerous prognostic sign for the child, since involvement in the custody proceedings is strongly correlated with later maladjustment (Wallerstein & Kelly, 1976, 1979). Klein and Westman's (1971) study of 105 families of divorce revealed that 52% had hostile postdivorce interactions requiring at least one court intervention and 31% required 2–10 court appearances in a 2-year follow-up. Some children engaged in the custody battle are permitted to read court transcripts and even testify on behalf of one parent. They are forced into a position of rejecting not only the other parent's behavior but also all those parts of that parent with which they had previously identified. For example, a boy who had an interest in soccer which he shared with his father may drop from the team despite his obvious enjoyment of the sport. This can be interpreted as internal splitting and can result in a decrease of self-worth.

Treatment

Custodial parents have a responsibility to help the child to see both sides. If they are not able to assist the child themselves, they should encourage the child to talk with a neutral adult. The child should be helped to appreciate that even though the parents are angry and hurt, this does not mean that the parents cannot accept the child's love for both. Occasionally it helps when the parents choose to discuss their anger and disappointment with a neutral third party. Sometimes this technique can avoid the guilt feelings of the children. Parents must insist on visiting, and the child, often despite expressed wishes, should be encouraged to maintain a close contact with the nonresident parent. Occasionally a child becomes angry at the custodial parent. In this instance, it appears to be safer for the child to be angry at the resident parent than to reject totally the nonresident parent. Occasionally these parent–child dyads are so intense that a paranoia exists in which the sense of reality is lost. The author recently saw the mother of a 9-year-old boy stop her son from visiting his father after the father bought a house and moved in with his girl friend. The mother was convinced that her husband was a sex maniac and that he and his girl friend were having sex in the living room while her son watched. The father and the boy previously enjoyed their weekends together. Michael would go to the lumberyard with his dad and help with minor renovations. The mother insisted on keeping her son from seeing his father even if it meant losing her son's self-respect. As a result, Michael became angry and critical of his father. Group therapy was recommended for Michael and counseling for both parents. In such a pathological interaction, it is easy to mistakenly identify the angry parent as severely disturbed and to focus treatment intervention on that parent. However, failure to include the nonresident parent in the counseling situation can often perpetuate the situation.

When a remarriage occurs, the anger that had been directed at the absent parent is often displaced onto the new marital partner. This can severely disrupt the integration of the reconstituted family. Preventative family therapy including all members of the reconstituted family is indicated, as well as counseling for the new couple with emphasis on parental control. In the absence of the second, buffer parent, frequently, older children are incorporated into the decision-making process by their custodial parent as an expedient to the managing of a household. When the parent remarries, however, there is a disruption to the reciprocal friend–confidante role (Weiss, 1979). The child struggles to maintain the homeostasis of the system after the remarriage. Family therapy is required to promote change.

ADOLESCENCE

Adolescent development can be divided into three subphases (Golombek, Wilkes, & Froese, 1977). Early adolescence is initiated and indicated by the growth spurt. It is characterized by temporary disorganization and a decreased willingness to accommodate the expectations of parents. Blos (1963) describes this as a letting go of the primary loved objects with an increase in narcissism and autoeroticism. Cognitively, young adolescents begin formal operations and abstract reasoning. Thus adolescents have adult intellectual and moral understanding. However, psychologically, they regress to a narcissistic stage. The adolescent has wide mood swings and periodic bouts of feeling ill-treated and unloved. Group activities are primarily with the same sex.

In midadolescence, the teenager is oriented more toward peer-centered activities. This is a stage characterized by adolescent rebellion with wide mood swings and rapidly changing feelings. Obedience to parental rules is replaced by conformity to the peer group. Early heterosexual exploration begins. Blos (1963) describes the detachment of psychic energy from the parental influence. He indicates that this process of detachment is accompanied by a sense of isolation equivalent to mourning.

Late adolescence is a period of transition. The adolescent, establishing self-identity and autonomy, states, "I want to be understood." Able to be more discriminating in relationships, the adolescent feels complete—a separate person, ready to maintain intimate relationships.

Sorosky (1977) found that parental divorce in the adolescent years can intensify adolescent conflicts, serve as a means of inhibiting expression and resolution, or stimulate a premature attempt at mastery. Wallerstein and Kelly (1974) describe this as pseudoadolescence. In a 4-year follow-up study of 21 adolescents, they found that the divorce process may force the adolescent to "de-idealize" the parent at an earlier stage than is developmentally desirable. Feelings of despair, anger, guilt, and depression may result when the parent demands that the child align himself with one parent or the other. "My sister was only seven years old so it was up to me to keep on the tough side but I was angry on the inside and I took my anger out on my little sister." Allison goes on to tell how trying to keep independent and distant from the conflict caused her to run away five or six times. "I would always come back. It was silly. I took sides. I was a brat and a bully. I never knew what it was going to be like. I had no understanding even though I expected it."

Westman (1970), reviewing the subjective questionnaires of 780 students who were representative of the general population in socioeconomic, housing, origin, and education, found that one sixth of the group were from divorced or separated families. This group showed less psychosomatic illness, less delinquent behavior, and better adjustment to both parents than children from unhappy, intact families. Nevertheless, they were not functioning as well as children from happy, intact homes. In a sample of 28 adolescents, self-defined as coping well with the divorce process, 2 out of 5 said that their parents were bitter and angry.

However, having achieved a level of cognitive development, the teenagers seemed to have an understanding of their parents' individual human differences. Many of the adolescents reported an improved relationship with each parent following separation (Robson, 1979).

If it comes at the right time, divorce can act as a spurt or an acceleration of growth toward maturity. Indeed, many adolescents report that they take on more responsibility than their peers. Duncan says, "Sometimes I think that people who go through divorce are lucky. I know you go through the hassles, but you learn so much how to cope with people and life in general. You learn how to take care of yourself more. You are more mature than other people. I don't need anyone to tell me what to do. I behave more responsibly. You learn to be more disciplined."

Phases in Coping

In interviewing adolescents from 11 to 18 years of age whose parents had separated after their 10th birthday and who reported that they were coping well with the separation, several phases of the process were identified. First, they reported that they were shocked but not surprised when the separation occurred. They knew it was coming for some time. Margaret says, "Oh wow. I know my parents are splitting up—something's really going on and I don't know what I am going to do. I talked a lot to my friends. Then suddenly it happened. I think I was so shocked when it did happen I was brainwashed. My mother told me absolutely everything that was going on. As far as I'm concerned, nobody should know." The stage of shock appears closely followed by a sense of relief that the family tension is over.

Within 2 days to 3 months afterward, the adolescents have an early acceptance of the permanence of the separation, despite one parent's desire to reunite. This early acceptance appears to be out of synchronism with the parents who are still coping with a sense of shock, disbelief, and loss. This initial precipitous acceptance of the separation by adolescents led many early investigators to assert that these children coped extremely well with little evidence of distress and pain during the process of divorce. Kurdek (1981) reminds us that findings for both parents and children need to be coordinated.

This early acceptance may be followed by anger. Adolescents, unlike their younger siblings, tend to become angry, not in reaction to which parent, if either, is culpable, but at a parent who is blaming or undermining the other parent. They experience a sense of loss of family life, often take on the family worries, and may develop pseudoparenting relationships with their own parents as well as experience intense loyalty conflicts. Adolescent symptomatology may not appear until 10 to 11 months following the initial separation. With their final acceptance of the situation, they report feeling more mature than their friends. Westman (1970) reports that divorce of parents of adolescents does not affect the adolescent's character formation but risks long-term effects on self-image. He notes that because adolescents go outside the home for comfort, advice, and nurturance, they are apt to perpetuate early marriage and subsequent divorce. However, the seeking of comfort outside the home may be protection for the adolescent, in that separation from the conflict protects them from overinvolvement with one or the other parent's argument.

Anthony (1974) noted that the initial reaction of the adolescents to the marriage breakup is grief accompanied by guilt. He goes on to describe the neurosis of abandonment in which every new relationship is approached apprehensively with the expectation of being rejected. Along with the sense of abandonment and guilt, Schwartzberg (1980), in a study of adolescent psychiatric patients, reports immediate reactions of disappointment and guilt. However, those adolescents who felt they were coping well denied any sense of guilt. Most respond as Marion does, "I don't see any reason to feel guilty. They got divorced. I felt no guilt at 13. Little kids don't understand emotions, sex, and things. Adolescents know about people. Obviously guilt is an immediate reaction for a little kid. It is very simple. Adolescents realize more about relationships."

Treatment

The adolescent demands and has the right to expect a great deal of external firmness and consistency in discipline. Custodial parents, regardless of their relationship with their children, were reported by their adolescents as inconsistent and too relaxed in disciplining. Adolescents who reported having increased freedom, less deadlines, and much more independent decision making missed the discipline and acutely felt this lack as a lack of caring on the part of parents. Jim says, "I think the loss of discipline is a loss, too. You know sometimes when I call on a friend to go to a party or something, his father and mother are always sitting there. 'Where are you going? Who is this person you are going with?' They always say, 'what time are you coming home?' He says '12:30,' his father says, '11:30.' It's always an hour earlier. We go out and it's kind of strange because I can stay out as late as I want but I feel like they're telling me too. I kind of miss it.'' Lack of discipline sometimes is reflected in a lower self-image as described by Santrock and Warshak (1979).

Adolescents, because of their developmental stage, appear to accept advice and direction not only from adults but from their peers. They tend to seek the advice of friends who have also experienced parental divorce. This tendency has led to the development of treatment modalities of peer counseling groups as a treatment of choice for adolescents. These groups are moderately structured and time limited. Because of the structure, the groups, unlike traditional psychotherapy groups, can include children from ages 10 to 18. The groups must be confidential and free from parental influence, although there is not counterindication to siblings being in the same group.

The use of creative drama as described by Barsky and Moyenter (1976) in the group program facilitates the expression of fantasy and feelings as well as reality-bound concepts. When creative drama is combined with videotape playback, the observing ego function of the group is enhanced and the emotions are emphasized. During the creative drama, parents are often objects of projection, portrayed as mean, selfish, abusive, and violent. Ultimately, the parents emerge as having strengths as well as weaknesses. Certain themes are common in adolescent peer counseling groups. Anxiety-charged issues include marital infidelity and family violence. Fear is expressed about parents' dating, and there is anxiety about parents who are not socially active. Although the adolescents experience an increased sense of responsibility and guilt if the parent is not socially active, when the parent expresses a wish to remarry the adolescent is concerned about having to move from the adult position that he or she currently occupies in the family back into a child role. In addition, in group therapy anxieties about homosexuality are often expressed. Although this is a normal fear during the adolescent development struggle, it appears to be increased during the divorce–remarriage period. Fears are expressed about disturbed gender identity formation as a result of living with only one parent, particularly if that parent has preferred an opposite-sex child. Not being of the preferred gender is an issue for adolescents of both sexes in the group. Discussion of loyalties is predominant in group sessions when holidays are imminent, especially summer and Christmas.

Young adolescent girls who have experienced the effect of father absence sometimes adopt attention-seeking behavior toward males and are at times promiscuous. Adolescent boys tend to act in a more aggressive manner. In these instances, individual psychotherapy is recommended. In some cases residential treatment may be required for the protection of the adolescent.

CONCLUSION

As the divorce rate increases and elementary schools report increasing percentages of students living in single-parent homes or in reconstituted families, the development of preventative programming for children is essential. This is necessary to avoid later maladaptive patterns.

Since children's reaction to separation and divorce appears to be specific to the developmental phase, it is important that teachers, counselors, lawyers, mental health professionals, and others who come into contact with them during the process of separation be attuned to these developmentally related symptoms. Primary prevention for development of later maladjustment and psychopathology can be accomplished through education of parents and by providing educational programs within the school system. When symptoms are present, treatment should be focused on the particular individual's need and oriented to the developmental stage of the child or adolescent.

REFERENCES

Als, H., Tronick, E., & Brazelton, T.B. Analysis of face-to-face interaction in infant-adult dyads. In M.E. Lamb, S.J. Suomi, & A.R. Stephenson (Eds.). *The study of social interaction.* Madison: University of Wisconsin Press, 1979.

Anthony, J. Children at risk from divorce: A review. In A. Koupernik and C. Koupernik (Eds.), *The child in his family: Children at a psychiatric risk.* New York: John Wiley, 1974, pp. 461–477.

Barsky, M., & Moyenter, A. The use of creative drama in a children's group. *International Journal of Group Psychotherapy,* 1976, *26,* 105–114.

Blos, P. *On adolescence.* New York: Free Press, 1963.

Glick, P.C. Children of divorced parents in demographic perspective. *Journal of Social Issues,* 1979, *35*(4), 170–182.

Golombek, H., Wilkes, J., & Froese, A.P. The developmental challenges of adolescence. In P.D. Steinhauer & Q. Rae-Grant (Eds.), *Psychological problems of the child and his family.* Toronto: Macmillan, 1977.

Hetherington, E.M., Cox, M., & Cox, R. Family interactions and the social, emotional and cognitive development of children following divorce. In J.C. Vaughan & T.B. Brazelton (Eds.), *The family: Setting priorities.* New York: Science & Medicine, 1979.

Jacobson, D.S. The impact of marital separation on children: III. Parent–child communication and child adjustment and regression analysis of findings from overall study. *Journal of Divorce,* 1978, *2*(2), 185–194.

Kelly, J., & Wallerstein, J. The effects of parental divorce: Experience of the child in early latency. *American Journal of Orthopsychiatry*, 1976, *46*, 20–21.

Klein, D.W., & Westman, J.C. The impact of divorce on the family. *Child's Psychiatry and Human Development*, 1971, *2*, 78–83.

Kurdek, L.A. An integrative perspective on children's divorce adjustment. *American Psychologist*, 1981, *36*, 856–866.

McDermott, J.F. Parental divorce in early childhood. *American Journal of Psychiatry*, 1968, *124*, 1424–1432.

Robson, B. *My parents are divorced, too*. New York: Everest House, 1979.

Rutter, M. Parent–child separation: Psychological effects on the children. *Journal of Child Psychology and Psychiatry*, 1971, *12*, 233–260.

Santrock, J.W., & Warshak, R.A. Father custody and social development in boys and girls. *Journal of Social Issues*, 1979, *35*, 112–125.

Schwartzberg, A. Adolescent reactions to divorce. In S.C. Feinstein et al. (Eds.), *Adolescent psychiatry: Developmental and clinical studies* (Vol. 3). University of Chicago Press, 1980.

Sorosky, A. The psychological effects of divorce on adolescents. *Adolescence*, 1977, *12*, 123–136.

Wallerstein, J.S., & Kelly, J. The effects of parental divorce: The adolescent experience. In E.F. Anthony & C. Koupernik (Eds.), *The child in his family: Children at psychiatric risk*. New York: Wiley, 1974.

Wallerstein, J.S., & Kelly, J.B. The effects of parental divorce: Experiences of the preschool child. *Journal of the American Academy of Child Psychiatry*, 1975, *14*, 600–616.

Wallerstein, J.S., & Kelly, J.B. The effects of parental divorce: Experiences of the child in later latency. *American Journal of Orthopsychiatry*, 1976, *46*, 256–269.

Wallerstein, J.S., & Kelly, J.B. Children and divorce: A review. *Social Work*, 1979, *24*, 468–475.

Weiss, R.S. *Going it alone*. New York: Basic Books, 1979.

Westman, J.C. Role of child psychiatry in divorce. *Archives of General Psychiatry*, 1970, *23*, 416–420.

Wilkinson, G.S., & Bleck, R.T. Children's divorce groups. *Elementary School Guidance and Counseling*, 1976, *11*, 205–213.

Winnicott, D.W. Transitional objects and transitional phenomena. *International Journal of Psychoanalysis*, *34*, 1–9 (Reprinted in *Collected papers by D.W. Winnicott (1958)*. London: Tavistock Publications, 1953).

6. The Supportive Separation System: A Joint Legal and Marital Counseling Alternative

Mario D. Bartoletti, Ed.D.
Bartoletti Consultants
Scarborough, Ontario, Canada

Patricia Bourke, S.S.W.
Bartoletti Consultants
Scarborough, Ontario, Canada

Ellen M. Macdonald, LLB.
Bartoletti Consultants
Scarborough, Ontario, Canada

Six

THE INAPPROPRIATENESS OF THE TRADITIONAL ADVERSARIAL approach for dealing with marital and family issues has been well documented, as has the traditional suspicion and attitudinal bias that characterizes much of the relationship between the legal and marital counseling professions. However, over the past decade, a variety of initiatives have been taken individually and jointly by the two professions designed to reduce the emotional wear and tear on couples who are separating or divorcing.

One such approach is the supportive separation system (SSS). Marital counseling aspects of the SSS were developed and tested by Bartoletti and Bourke between 1971 and 1977 at the Family Life Center in Markham, Ontario. Legal aspects of the SSS were developed and explored independently by Macdonald between 1977 and 1981 in her private practice in Toronto, Ontario.

THE MARITAL COUNSELING PERSPECTIVE

From the outset the SSS was designed to provide four major components:

1. a foundation that would provide an opportunity for strong tripartite collaboration and cooperation of the marital counseling profession, the legal profession, and the couple;
2. a means whereby the couple would assume greater responsibility and control over the resolution of separation issues;

3. an alternative offering greater trust between both marital partners and between both professions; and
4. a written contract or agreement clarifying the respective responsibilities and benefits for both partners.

A key tenet of the SSS approach is the ongoing involvement of the marital counselor beyond the point at which reconciliation counseling has come to an end. Traditionally, once marital counseling has been perceived as being unsuccessful in continuing the marital arrangement, the counselor has stepped aside and the couple has sought legal assistance to arrange a separation. In effect, the traditional approach removes a trusted and knowledgeable support when both partners are most vulnerable to anxiety, suspicion, and anger. The couple then becomes involved with the legal and judicial systems, providing a determined adversarial stance that effectively dissolves whatever emotional support the two partners could offer each other and displaces it with separate legal representation that often ruptures the couple's positive interpersonal communicating and relating processes.

To counter those retrograde procedures, the SSS approach maintains regular counselor involvement. It is acknowledged that "when the marital relationship breaks down, the need for conciliation between husband and wife actually increases as they prepare to live apart (Bartoletti, 1974, p. 4). However, for the marital counselor to be effective, his or her role must change from attempting to keep the partners together to helping them move apart. In turn, the partners require considerable assistance in adjusting to the new, unexpected, and usually painful direction of separating themselves and dividing the family.

That process, termed the *repositioning sequence,* requires delicate and sensitive handling. It is best done before any legal involvement. When accomplished with care, repositioning can provide significant movement toward a successful emotional adjustment to the separation by both parents, their children, and other extended family members. It also establishes an atmosphere of trust, which is extended by the partners from their trust in the counselor to increased trust in themselves and each other. In turn, the way is eased toward discussing the major aspects of the written separation agreement. The process of repositioning clients presupposes that the marital counselor has explored the marital situation and has assessed the clients' expectations and needs, their individual positions as marriage partners, and their dissatisfactions. This familiarity with the clients is essential to the process. Bearing in mind that the differing emotional makeups of the two partners emerge during counseling plus the fact that they seldom move in the same direction or at the same speed invariably leaves one reaching the point of discussing a possible separation ahead of the other. The former is referred to as the *initiator,* the latter, as the *respondent.*

Another important aspect of repositioning that has to be considered in the situation of separation is that parenting, rather than being a result of the proximity and unconscious expectations of living together as a couple, has to become a consciously shared concern requiring thorough discussion and careful arrangements. The degree of dependence one partner has had for the other often becomes a topic for intense discussion. How realistic the dependence was and how such needs will be met after separation is an area that requires close examination and often concrete suggestions.

For the counselor, the change of focus from marriage counseling to the separation of a couple means dealing with new disappointment, new fear, newly dashed hopes, and the sense of failure. The respondent client often sees the counselor as having taken sides, sometimes as even being partly to blame for the breakdown of the marriage counseling. There is a sense that somehow the cause of the separation was the counselor's acceptance of such an alternative. When both the initiator and respondent can involve themselves with the counselor in resolving that initial misperception and when the blaming can be seen by both as merely a natural attempt to avoid the pain of separation, then repositioning begins. The counseling focus then becomes one of looking at those areas that will continue to be of mutual concern to the wife and husband and deciding how those are to be handled. The process is one of supportive acknowledgment of individual strengths and vulnerabilities. The disappointment concerning the past and the immobilizing fear of the future must be constantly balanced by refocusing on the realistic needs and resources of the present. Recurring grief can be replaced by a sense of relief as the respondent realizes that the family is not being abandoned. The initiator can experience a similar sense of relief with the realization that there is no need to abandon the partner and fight for a period of separation.

The mutual concerns must include the emotional and economic survival of both partners and the preservation of a life style for the children conducive to their intellectual and emotional development. Partners who have successfully repositioned themselves or who emotionally engage in the process begin to deal with each other with a respect that is implemented in the planning for the survival of each other as parents and as individuals. The wife who makes a list of the basic household items that her husband will need and may take from the marital home and the husband who makes himself available to look after the children while his wife engages in retraining for the job market are examples of the kind of caring that spring to mind. "Since both partners can benefit from a breathing space, during which some healing and restoration of jangled nerves can begin, both partners have a stake in working together to arrange such a separation agreement" (Bartoletti, 1975, p. 3).

Separation Agreement Proposal

To a significant degree, the repositioning sequence is very important to the contracting process in which the couple then engages with the goal of successfully completing a separation agreement *proposal*. The repositioning sequence is designed to forestall the many myths and misconceptions that cause great anxiety to laypersons. As Kronby (1972) puts it so well: "They hear third-hand and usually exaggerate stories of the complexity and cost of divorce proceedings. They are intimidated by the prospects of having to appear in court, and put off by technical legal language" (p. 7). Naturally, as they come to understand that the separation process can be completed without court intervention, with communications using language they can understand, both partners usually can then proceed with much of their anxiety reduced.

Within such a revised approach to separation, the partners are assisted in understanding the natural progression of alternatives open to them:

a. the SSS;
b. the traditional adversarial approach; and
c. the courts.

An important aspect to keep in mind about the three steps (and which is made clear to the couple) is that of control. The first step leaves almost total control and the terms of the separation agreement in the hands of the two partners. The latter two steps move toward an erosion of their control—in and of itself a recognition by the couple that they have not been able to negotiate an agreement without the need for increased guidance and direction imposed from the outside. The traditional adversarial approach is an arrangement in which the two partners no longer deal directly with each other—leaving much of the negotiating in the hands of their respective lawyers. Moving to the courts leaves the final decisions in the hands of a judge.

It is felt by many in the marital counseling and legal professions that the majority of separating couples can handle their separation issues with the first alternative. However, for those couples who cannot, the other two alternatives will continue to be available.

Within the SSS, one of the primary functions of the marital counselor is to assist the couple in drawing up their proposal for a separation agreement, arriving at terms with which both are comfortable and in language both can easily understand. The guidelines, developed in consultation with family lawyers and family court judges, are based on the practical need to avoid unnecessary conflict at a time when both partners are at a fragile point in their relationship.

First, the agreement proposal is usually arranged for a temporary period of 6 months, thus reducing the natural anxiety about signing for an indefinite period of time. It is done in recognition of the fact that separation is not necessarily a first step toward divorce; it is a transition point, a way station where a couple and their family can pause for a while before making the larger decision of trying it again together, or perhaps moving toward divorce proceedings. Second, because it is for a temporary period, sale of the family home and formal division of the joint assets are discouraged unless serious financial need makes such arrangements absolutely necessary. This eliminates the need for extensive, often perilous financial negotiations. Third, continuing joint custody of the children is strongly encouraged to give both partners the opportunity to maintain meaningful involvement with their parental responsibilities. Such an arrangement can often remove the whole parent–child area of potential conflict from what is basically a problem between husband and wife. That, in turn, usually facilitates negotiations around where the children will be residing, child support, and visitation arrangements with them (Brown, 1981). Fourth, the couple is encouraged to maintain contact with the counselor during the separation period to forestall possible emotional depression and deterioration in the conciliative stance which they have achieved with each other.

Legal Consultation

Once the separation agreement proposal has been completed and the counselor and the couple feel reasonably assured that most of the emotional areas of conflict have been satisfactorily handled along with the specific terms negotiated, then referral to lawyers can be made. It is common within the SSS approach for the couple to approach the legal profession with the main points of the separation agreement effectively settled and their emotional state significantly stabilized. A close cooperative relationship between the marital counselor and the lawyers assists in maintaining that stabilization.

One lawyer within the SSS functions as a legal consultant to both the wife and husband, but represents neither because the wife and husband are not in conflict. The lawyer reviews the separation agreement proposal, and then, with the couple, explains the terms of their proposal à propos the various laws and acts that may apply. The lawyer's job is facilitated because the couple is ready emotionally to deal with the legal implications more calmly and objectively than is otherwise often the case.

The same points hold true should the couple elect to arrange for separate legal consultation. By working closely with the marital counselor, both lawyers know that they have an ally and colleague familiar with the couple's sensitivities should emotional problems requiring counseling intervention arise.

It is reassuring to the couple to know that their marital counseling and legal consultants are working closely together. (There is also one important advantage in having each partner consult with his or her own lawyer. Should a conflict arise between the marital partners that they cannot resolve even with the marital counselor's assistance, then each partner would continue to be represented by his or her lawyer during litigation. In instances in which one lawyer is consulting with both partners, that lawyer cannot ethically represent either partner in the event of conflict— and would have to withdraw from the case.)

By actively assisting the couple throughout the repositioning sequence and the phases of working through a separation agreement proposal in layman's language, the marital counselor knows that the introduction of legal assistance can be accomplished without the suspicion and hostility common to the traditional adversarial approach. In turn, the lawyer can work with the couple supportively, advising on legal issues and finalizing the separation agreement without resorting to the costly intervention of the court. Regular contact between the marital counselor and the lawyer can usually provide the guidance and direction that the couple might need.

THE LEGAL PERSPECTIVE

The SSS as described herein is based on a recognition that the traditional adversarial approach, when used by lawyers in solving problems of persons facing marital breakdown, is inappropriate for several reasons. However, from the point of view of the legal profession there would be a reluctance to suddenly alter the traditional approach to resolve family law disputes. This sudden alteration is made in the face of a long-established tradition of resorting to the adversarial processes not only in extreme circumstances but also when the prevailing threat of the intervention of the adversarial approach is a constant one. In other words, lawyers are frequently inclined to say to each other that if the matter is unresolvable, "then let a court decide."

The professional training and background of lawyers is a significant factor that has to be taken into account when one looks at the inappropriateness of the traditional adversarial system. Lawyers, by virtue of their training, are naturally inclined to think in terms of resolving problems in a win-or-lose perspective. Persons who seek the assistance of lawyers tend to become immediately polarized and to start a process of lining up against each other, creating an air of distrust and combativeness carried on not only between the lawyers but also between the participating clients.

This tendency is further complicated at the present time by the vast numbers of lawyers entering the field in times of economic stress, with the result that some judgment, which might otherwise be directed toward expeditious and early resolution of problems, is clouded because of an awareness that extended negotiations or litigation results in, among other things, extended professional fees.

It is interesting to note that with respect to the latter problem, the Supreme Court of Ontario has recognized this tendency and is now operating with substantial changes to the rules of court. These changes are directed toward the conduct of litigants and the impact of this conduct on the matter of costs in legal proceedings. The result is that persons who take unreasonable positions in matrimonial disputes are liable for the costs of the other party who has been put to the unnecessary legal expense.

There is also an attitudinal bias between lawyers and members of the counseling professions that has existed for a long time. This bias, founded or unfounded, on either side, has made it extremely difficult for both professional groups to work effectively in solving the problems of their clients or patients. Lawyers tend to resent what they consider to be the encroachment by counselors into areas of the technical application of the law. At the same time, marital counselors become resentful of what they perceive to be the negative impact of lawyers on any progress that the counselors have had in resolving the couple's problems in a conciliative manner.

LAWYER–COUNSELOR RELATIONSHIPS

So that lawyers and counselors may understand each other and each other's methods, the Toronto-based group of Bartoletti, Bourke, and Macdonald has been developing a formal process whereby lawyers and counselors could benefit from each other's skills. So far, the Toronto group has received positive responses from the two professions. (This is not to state, of course, that no persons from the professional groups are skeptical about the supportive separation system.) To continue developing their ideas, Bartoletti, Bourke, and Macdonald are soliciting the input of interested professionals for the establishment of a professional association that would provide for a professional training institute directed toward expanding the conciliatory approach for the resolution of marital disputes. The training program ideally would not only teach mediation skills to both professions but would also be a skills exchange whereby marital counselors would become more attuned to legal skills (particularly in the face of complex amendments to existing legislation), and lawyers would become more attuned to counseling skills, which would, in turn, help them be sensitive to the complexities of interpersonal behavior in marital breakdown.

As an example, Macdonald is of the view that she has benefited greatly through her personal participation in several training programs in the United States directed toward successful mediation and conciliation. She is hopeful that similar programs could be developed and become available to family law lawyers in Canada.

At the present time there are an increasing number of lawyers who are prepared to enter into negotiations in family law disputes with the degree of delicacy that is essential for the parties to resolve their differences without continued distrust, hatred, or other ill feeling toward the initiating or respondent spouse, as the case may be. In Toronto, lawyers are recognizing the positive aspects of mediation, counseling, and conciliation. Significant steps have been taken by the legal profession to educate lawyers on the desirability of this approach. A divorce mediation group is active in the Canadian Bar Association's Family Law Section. Where clients desire a conciliation process it can be arranged, provided that there is cooperation between the lawyers and the courts. In cases where conciliation is recognized and desired by both parties the courts are most anxious to assist in any manner to make use of conciliation methods.

The use of conciliation and mediation has had a positive impact on the relationship between lawyers and counselors in that lawyers are now realizing that counselors do play an effective role in resolving disputes. As long as no professional group attempts to encroach upon the technical areas of the other's expertise, a model that encompasses lawyers and counselors working together is a desirable one. Accordingly, the Toronto group's efforts toward the formation of an inter-professional association will facilitate closer cooperation between lawyers and counselors, provide for the appropriate exchange of skills, and make available a much more practical, efficient service for couples contemplating separation.

Of paramount importance to the overall success of the SSS is the realization by all participants that it must be understood that at no time will a participant's legal rights be prejudiced. In particular, before any final formal separation agreement is executed by either party, it will be reviewed separately by a lawyer of each person's choice. In this manner, the hazard of using the services of one lawyer is recognized and met, with the result that the goal of reaching a formal separation agreement that can withstand the passage of time, as far as it is possible to do so, is achieved. Whatever future dissatisfactions there may be, they will not arise from an allegation that there was coercion or some other unawareness that led to the signing of a separation agreement. Once an agreement is reached, both parties realize that the resolution by way of agreement is more satisfactory than by use of the judicial process. When a judge makes a decision within the realm of the existing legal framework, there is usually a perception that the disposition of the matter, whatever it may be, is a rather arbitrary one. In addition to the dissatisfaction that comes as a result of the perception of arbitrariness, there is the reality of the financial consequences of the legal processes, which include costly pretrial proceedings in the nature of examinations for discovery, cross-examinations, interlocutory motions, and a trial. This expense becomes enormous. The bitterness that develops as a result of the victor-vanquished attitude is usually also lifelong.

At the same time, it must always be recognized that in certain situations there are facts and circumstances that dictate that there is no reasonable alternative but to use the adversarial approach. These cases are in the minority, as the Supreme Court of Ontario statistics clearly bear out. The SSS places the marital counselor and the lawyer closer together and establishes a more practical and positive arrangement for interprofessional trust, cooperation, and exchange of skills. The primary beneficiaries to this approach are the clients, but, ultimately, both professions, the courts, and society at large will benefit.

CONCLUSION

The SSS provides an integrated network of marital counseling and legal skills that involves a separating couple in a cooperative rather than adversarial approach. It picks up immediately after reconciliation efforts have broken down and effectively provides a positive alternative for working toward a separation agreement. The majority of couples electing to separate are able to maintain a constructive approach when provided with practical support from the professionals on whom they rely.

A further advantage of the SSS approach is that it effectively bridges the gap between the breakdown of reconciliation efforts and the conciliative efforts of divorce mediation usually available through the court clinics attached to the family courts. The philosophical goals of the supportive separation and divorce mediation groups are similar, as indicated by Irving (1980): "A major goal of divorce mediation is to help the couple become rational and responsible enough to cooperate towards making compromises which are acceptable to both people. Voluntary settlements, worked out by the spouses on both an emotional level as well as an intellectual one are not only more humane than those forced by litigation, but they are also more practical."

By integrating the SSS approach with the court clinics, couples and their families can be assisted through a second repositioning sequence to consider movement toward a divorce, should that be desired by the couple. Supportive separation also places the marital counselor and the lawyer closer together by establishing an early practical and positive arrangement for interprofessional trust and cooperation. If all of this could be achieved, the professional roles of both groups would not only be considerably easier but far more rewarding.

REFERENCES

Bartoletti, M.D. Separation: Perspective on the couple, the counselor and the lawyer. *The Single Parent Journal*, 1974, *17*(7), 4-6.

Bartoletti, M.D. Separation is a time for working together. *The One Parent Family Journal*, 1975, *1*(2), 2-3.

Brown, L. The cost of loving: Inflation hits alimony. *Toronto Star*, July 23, 1981, p. #1.

Irving, H. *Divorce mediation*. Toronto: Personal Library, 1980.

Kronby, M.C. *The guide to family law*. Toronto: New Press, 1972.

7. Toward a Structural Theory of Family Mediation

Lawrence D. Gaughan, J.D.
Attorney-at-Law
Arlington, Virginia

Seven

MEDIATION IS NOT A NEW MODE OF HUMAN INTERACTION. The idea of a mediator—a third person in the middle—is as old as the need of human civilization to settle disputes in a civilized manner. There are only two ways in which disputes can peacefully be resolved; between the participants unassisted and through the intercession of one or more third parties. If the third party's role is to foster effective negotiation between the disputants, then the process is called mediation.

The new element in mediation is its application to resolving the legal incidents of separation and divorce. Of particular novelty is the development of family mediation as a discrete professional field, which has occurred in the United States only during the past 5 years.

Family mediation centers on the necessary matters that a couple must resolve in a separation or divorce. These include a division of their marital property, allocation of responsibilities toward their children, and any transfer of funds for support. The mediator needs to know of the criteria for, and the parameters of, judicial intervention if a settlement cannot be negotiated. The mediator also must have a basic knowledge of other possible implications (including taxes) of any options that the parties may consider.

An attorney mediator may possess a clinical understanding of the skills of effective negotiation and will probably be aware of the different levels of generality at which agreement can be achieved and implemented. But mediation is not the practice of law. The mediator generally refrains from suggesting substantive solutions, relying instead on the parties' assent to the mediators' control of the process.

Nor is mediation therapy, even though a therapist mediator may do a kind of mediation in marriage or family therapy. The closest analogy is to conjoint divorce counseling, which is too seldom practiced. A therapist mediator may have a knowledge of the nature of the emotional interactions of the couple and be skilled in techniques for resolution of the emotional blockages. A therapist may also have the ability to assist individuals in reaching mature decisions.

Therapists and lawyers usually do not have any explicit training in conflict resolution. Both have clinical experience in the divorce process, but often this focuses on what appears as pathology in the couple's interactions. There is too often an assumption that an emotionally enmeshed couple going through separation or divorce is a hopeless case for a reasoned, fair settlement. Recent developments in the field of conflict resolution may thus add a dimension to the professional practice of attorneys and therapists who do family mediation.

DYSFUNCTIONAL BEHAVIOR PATTERNS

In several senses, of course, conflict is at the heart of any therapeutic structure. Psychoanalytic psychotherapy focuses on intrapsychic conflict as a generative source of anxiety. Family systems therapy furnishes various models for dealing with the anxiety resulting from interpersonal relationships.

Wherever its roots are found in the past or present, conflict is central to every approach to human psychology. Self or other is the tension at the core of every relationship. The manner in which conflict arises and is dealt with is a basic issue in every human system.

Every marriage either stagnates or otherwise becomes dysfunctional, or grows and thrives, depending on the couple's creativity (or lack of it) in managing conflict. If the spouses can negotiate effectively with each other, then the marriage will stay together or, if there is a divorce, they may be able to retain a good relationship. If their negotiations are ineffective, then their conflict will be handled less functionally.

The more the interactions of wife and husband are governed by emotionality, the less likely they will be able to resolve their conflicts effectively. Their ability to negotiate is in inverse proportion to their level of emotional enmeshment, and the possibility of no resolution or dysfunctional resolution of ongoing conflict is elevated correspondingly.

One common dysfunctional approach to conflict is to avoid it. This may involve denial, rationalization, or intellectualization. Avoidance is perhaps the worst approach to conflict, since it is neither assertive nor cooperative. It preserves the conflict and, in some cases, provokes the other to respond in a reactive emotional manner. If the conflict is inappropriately smoothed over or diffused, there will be a later emotional backlash of some sort.

Accommodating the other is also dysfunctional, since it falsifies the conflict. One party gives in, or appears to give in. There is insufficient regard for one's own legitimate needs and goals. This may be related to defensiveness or guilt. The accommodation may be at only one level, as in a passive–aggressive reaction. Or it may be centered in an excessive dependency on the other. All of these responses are dysfunctional.

The alternative to flight (avoidance or accommodation) is fight. One confronts the conflict head on, either through anger or through a determination to compete in order to win. One discounts or puts down the other or, perhaps, retaliates or mounts an offensive to defeat the other. All of these, like the other dysfunctional responses, are the result of emotional reactivity.

Other keys to the emotional reactivity of a more enmeshed couple are poor listening, obsessing, playing games, and swings in position or mood. The entire relationship, rather than the specific issues to be settled, may appear to be in dispute. Enmeshment can be diagnosed when there is a disproportionate focus on minor issues or when no issue seems to stay settled. Another clue is lack of resolution of an apparent communication breakdown. Finally, an imbalance in negotiating skills in a couple is a sign that their relationship is uneven.

These dysfunctional patterns often become deeply engrained in a couple. There may even be physical or mental illness in one or both spouses. There are cases of husbands and wives who habitually withdraw emotionally from the other, or become physically ill, as a means of managing conflict in the marriage. Another pattern is that of the overresponsible and overdependent couple.

Patterns such as these can become fixed in some couples, so that any intervention that disrupts the dysfunctional system will raise, rather than lower, the anxiety level. Marital separation in an enmeshed couple will not radically alter the basic level of emotional enmeshment. The form of response to conflict may change drastically, however, as in the case where a passive–dependent, overly accommodating spouse seeks retaliation as an outlet for anger at the other's decision to separate.

THE MEDIATION PROCESS

From one perspective, the divorce process is the transition out of the emotional reactivity of the marriage. This transition may seem to take place at a different pace in each of the spouses. Usually this is explained by the fact that one spouse commenced the transition at an earlier point than the other, or that there has been a switch to some different form of emotional response to the conflict.

The challenge of family mediation is that it requires an ability to structure the interactions of the couple so that they can negotiate effectively. Often the spouses have not negotiated well during their marriage, which is one cause for their separation. Now, as their relationship is undergoing a drastic change, they are being asked to be fair and reasonable with each other.

The separation or divorce is a systemic change. But at an emotional level, the same approximate degree of reactivity may still be present. It is the need to settle property, support, and custody issues that makes possible more basic change between the couple. This becomes founded in some sort of emotional resolution that is reflected in the legal settlement or, perhaps, results from that agreement.

Mediation is a goal-directed process, but the goal (the legal agreement) is different from that of any form of therapy. The mediator keeps the discussion on target, supplies needed information, and otherwise controls the process. The structural task for the mediator is to maintain the negotiation of the spouses at a level where it is balanced and effective.

Negotiation is most effective when each party is in touch with his or her needs, entitlements (rights), and goals, as well as relevant values and beliefs. It requires a combination of positive assertiveness and cooperation. Assertiveness is responsibility for oneself, whereas cooperation is responsibility to the other. These attributes to the relationship will exist when each party can maintain a reasonable balance between the cognitive and emotional components.

Each spouse needs full and accurate information about income, property, assets, liabilities, and monthly expenses of the other. This permits each to negotiate for himself or herself, but with an appreciation for the needs and entitlements of the other. The relationship of the marriage is being transformed, at least in some ways, into a series of transactions through the legal agreement. But each party must acknowledge some obligation of fairness to the other resulting from the positive elements of their past relationship.

Effective negotiation meets mutual needs and is mutually beneficial. It does not rely excessively on power or coercion. Each party can appreciate that both positions have some validity within legitimate parameters taken in good faith. It is precisely this assumption of mutual validity that balances the negotiation and keeps the emotional component from becoming excessive. Collaboration, or at least compromise, then becomes possible.

Such a balance is possible when each member of the couple can accept two definitions of their relationship: (a) that they remain a family, despite the separation or divorce, and (b) that the family relationship has been, or will shortly be, permanently changed in its nature. Both elements are important because if they are mutually understood the spouses are less likely to negotiate at cross-purposes.

Effective negotiation requires a continuing focus on the task, a settlement that meets the financial, property, and parenting needs of both parties. The mutual goals of mediation include saving time and expense, avoiding the stress of litigation, dealing comprehensively with the issues, and reaching a flexible and satisfactory solution. A court only decides, but a couple in mediation can work at problem solving.

Therefore, the issue is not who is the better parent, but how the responsibilities toward the children may best be shared. It is not important who caused the separation, but rather what exchange of income and property will recognize the contributions of each to the marriage and meet their future separate needs. In the most difficult mediations, these formulations involve a kind of essential reframing.

Conflict resolution allows for focusing on the task as a way to manage the emotionality of the conflict. Once the issue is clarified, it may become possible to explore the concerns that may underlie a given position. Positions (''my side on this point'') are often undesirable in mediation because of the emotions attached to them. Concerns, on the other hand, are less threatening to discuss because it is easier to reflect on their content with some objectivity. There is also often less potential for conflict at the concern level because concerns are usually more general and flexible than the positions that they underlie.

MODEL OF COUPLES IN MEDIATION

The more emotionally enmeshed the couple is, the greater the need for a carefully formulated conflict resolution strategy. The reason for this is suggested by the model of couples in mediation to be set forth in Figure 1. This model was suggested by the circumplex model of family systems designed by Olson (1979). The adaptations to his model result from the integration of conflict resolution ideas in a relevant mediation structure.

Figure 1 portrays the cohesion and adaptability dimensions of a couple in mediation. It also assumes that in the divorce process, one or both members of the couple may move to a different point on the model. Usually, however, the movement is to the opposite side (especially on the cohesion dimension) rather than to the center. The center charts the ideal and is roughly equivalent to Bowen's (1978) concept of "differentiation." (See Figure 1.)

Figure 1 Emotional Patterns in Family Mediation

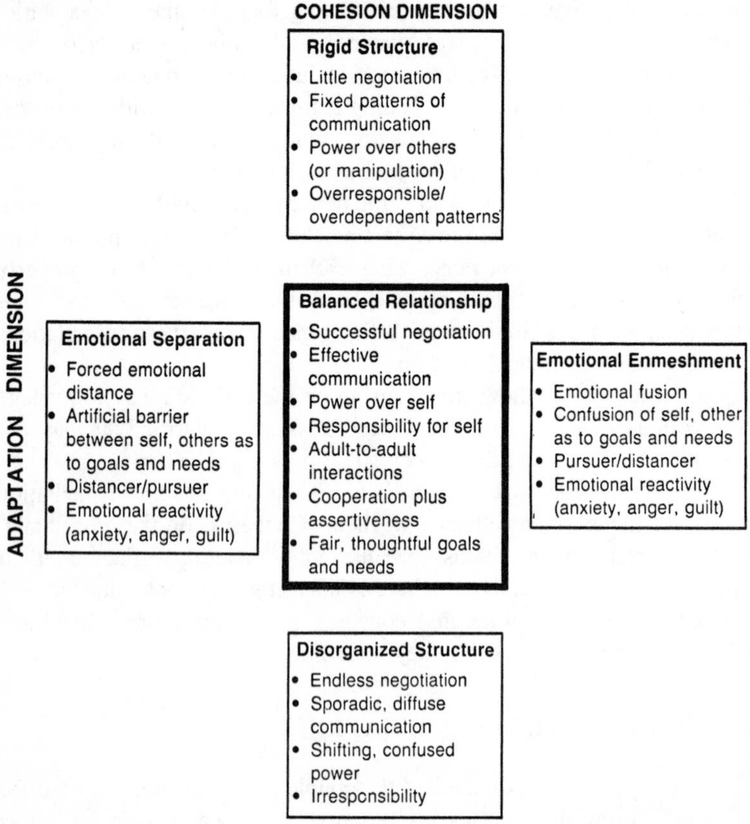

COHESION DIMENSION

Rigid Structure
- Little negotiation
- Fixed patterns of communication
- Power over others (or manipulation)
- Overresponsible/overdependent patterns

ADAPTATION DIMENSION

Emotional Separation
- Forced emotional distance
- Artificial barrier between self, others as to goals and needs
- Distancer/pursuer
- Emotional reactivity (anxiety, anger, guilt)

Balanced Relationship
- Successful negotiation
- Effective communication
- Power over self
- Responsibility for self
- Adult-to-adult interactions
- Cooperation plus assertiveness
- Fair, thoughtful goals and needs

Emotional Enmeshment
- Emotional fusion
- Confusion of self, other as to goals and needs
- Pursuer/distancer
- Emotional reactivity (anxiety, anger, guilt)

Disorganized Structure
- Endless negotiation
- Sporadic, diffuse communication
- Shifting, confused power
- Irresponsibility

If both members of the couple are near the center of the model, the mediation will probably be less difficult. The mediator will be able to spend more time on the technical issues such as tax options, equity trade-offs, and trust funds for the children. The couple may be able to decide many issues on their own, and generally they can do this effectively.

The further the spouses are from the center of the model, the higher their level of emotionality. Their style of negotiation may be directly conflictual, with threats, insults, and blaming. Or it may involve a pattern of dictating by one spouse and withdrawing by the other. Or there may be mutual attempts to manipulate each other. These are some of the commonly observed forms of pseudonegotiation used by couples in mediation.

A serious problem with the emotionally involved couple in mediation is that communication is poor. People have difficulty hearing each other when the emotional level is high. Effective communication consists of listening to what the other person is saying. At times it is necessary to have some ventilation of anger to achieve this. The mediator can set the tone of the interaction and work patiently on feedback models. Sometimes, role reversals are effective. Often, the mediator will need to repeat or rephrase statements.

With a deeply conflicted couple, there may be as little as 10 minutes of genuine negotiation in a 2-hour session. The mediator should have an easel available to make a permanent record of any elements of agreement reached during such a productive period. An easel is an absolutely essential tool for the most effective mediation in difficult cases.

Another resistant problem in mediation is that of withdrawal by one spouse. The conflict resolution style may be either avoidance or excessive accommodation. When dealing with avoidance, it is difficult to obtain agreement. With excessive accommodation, agreement may be reached rapidly, but it will not be fair. In either case, the mediator must be patient to draw out effective participation by the passive spouse. Again, the easel may be important as a means of encouraging both spouses to take part in a more objective way and to demonstrate the need for balance.

Usually the couple's style of negotiation is a key to the level of emotionality in their relationship. It is crucial that the mediator pay close attention to the ways in which each spouse seeks to influence the other. Often one observes techniques of negotiation that are extremely ineffective. One may also observe how, on occasion, ineffective ploys actually appear to succeed. And, of course, the mediator needs to be aware of how he or she influences the couple's negotiation process.

In difficult situations, the mediator may be tempted to manage the process by giving advice, making substantive recommendations, interpreting motivations or behavior, or directly confronting one or both spouses. One or more of these techniques may be useful on occasion, but their use should have better justification than as a release for the mediator's sense of frustration.

The process goal of mediation is to bring the couple to effective negotiation with each other by focusing on specific and practical issues. This can take place even with a deeply enmeshed couple. But generally this couple should be discouraged from negotiating without the mediator present. In terms of the model, the objective is to move them toward the center, if only during the mediation session. This may also assist them in generally restructuring their relationship as they move through the divorce process. But they will probably not be able to maintain any meaningful level of really effective negotiation for long.

One of the skills required by a mediator is the ability to teach. The best reference on negotiation is the recently published book, *Getting To Yes,* by Fisher and Ury (1981) of the Harvard Negotiation Project. One way to teach effective negotiation is to selectively demonstrate the way in which ineffective techniques fail to achieve their objective. This can be done with gentle humor if the mediator can use humor appropriately.

CONCLUSION

The structure and techniques of mediation are complex. This article has concentrated on a structure for understanding the tasks of mediation in terms of the patterns of emotional interaction in the couple. Comments on technique have been related to the postulated structure.

Although the structure originated in a family systems model, it evolved into a negotiations model. The emotional systems outside the model's center describe patterns of less effective negotiation. Negotiation is only one way to approach an understanding of family systems. It is much more basic to mediation.

REFERENCES

Bowen, M. *Family therapy in clinical practice*. New York: Jason Aronson, 1978.
Fisher, R., & Ury, W. *Getting to yes*. Boston: Houghton Mifflin, 1981.
Olson, D.H. Circumplex model of marital and family systems. *Family Process*, 1979, *18*, 3–28.

SUGGESTED READINGS

Deutsch, M. *The resolution of conflict*. New Haven, Conn.: Yale University Press, 1973.
Edinburg, G.M. *Clinical interviewing and counseling*. New York: Appleton-Century-Crofts, 1974.
Haynes, J.M. *Divorce mediation*. New York: Springer, 1981.
Kaslow, F.W. The stages of divorce: A psychological perspective. *Villanova Law Review*, 1979–80, *25*, 718–751.
Kressel, K. A typology of divorcing couples: Implications for mediation and the divorce process. *Family Process*, 1980, *19*, 101-116.

8. Stepfamilies in the 1980s

Emily B. Visher, Ph.D.
Stepfamily Association of America
Palo Alto, California

John S. Visher, M.D.
Adult Outpatient Services
North County Mental Health Center
Palo Alto, California

Eight

A letter arrives:
Please send any information or advice on how to contact the chapter (of Stepfamily Association of America) nearest to us. HELP!!. . . Between us we have five children: a son 18 years old, a daughter 14 years old, a son 13 years old, a daughter 12 years old, and a daughter 2½ years old. We have been married one month.

THIS SHORT LETTER CONVEYS CLEARLY AND SIMPLY THE complexity, the stress, and the anxiety that suddenly can appear when a remarriage between two people with children from a previous relationship takes place. In such a case there is no simple wedding with a quiet honeymoon. The ordinary adjustment period, with gradual changes in the family life cycle as children are born and slowly grow to maturity, is missing. Instead, there is instant chaos—marriage with five children at different stages of development, coming together to be with one another under one roof, not knowing what to expect next!

When a number of persons of varying ages and stages of development suddenly come together from a variety of previous family and household backgrounds, each one already has ideas about how the television set should be used, where the dog sleeps, who prepares the breakfast, how the laundry is folded, and how the hamburgers are cooked. The problem, of course, is that there is no agreement. Everyone brings different family traditions from their former family experiences—most of them givens below conscious awareness until the startling experiences of trying to mind a parent who allows watching television before dinner or finding the dog sleeping at the foot of the bed.

In addition, family alliances form, with outsiders and insiders vying for positions because of the parent–child relationships that preceded the new couple's relationship. An only child may suddenly have three sisters. A biological parent may remain in memory if not in actuality. The children may be members of at least two households—going back and forth, experiencing culture shock. A stepfamily is a complex family with a large cast of characters—a family forest rather than a family tree.

CULTURAL PRESSURES

Families do not exist in a vacuum. The cultural myths and expectations that surround stepfamilies complicate the period of transition and integration, which, to quote one stepmother, "doesn't take months, it takes *years.*"

Remarriage and recommitment is one phase of a process that starts after a divorce or the death of a parent, then moves through the single-parent household phase, and finally reaches the remarriage stage. What happens during each phase can be very important to the success of each succeeding phase. Cultural attitudes are important. Although society remains uncomfortable with divorce, the reaction prevalent several decades ago has changed, softening as divorce has become much more common, especially during the decade of the 1970s. Support groups for divorced and separated parents have grown out of society's recognition of the pain and loss involved, as well as the financial and emotional burden carried by single parents caring for their children. Coparenting agreements and joint custody arrangements are recent attempts to ease the trauma and relationship loss for both the children and the adults.

Attention has been given to studying the effects of divorce on the children (Wallerstein & Kelly, 1980). There is a growing recognition that, for the mental health of the children, no parent is disposable. Eighty percent of divorced persons remarry within 4 to 5 years, and 60% of them have children. When remarriage occurs and a stepfamily is born, it is out of the losses of the past. Unfortunately, the cultural expectation often is that once again, almost miraculously and instantaneously, a family as well integrated as the original one has been created. There is often a failure to realize that a stepfamily is a new and different family type with its own complexities and structure. The ideal American family is traditionally biological, consisting of a mother, a father, two children, and two sets of grandparents. The attempt by the adults in many step-families to fit their new household into this mold leads to unrealistic expectations, frustration, resentments, and pain for all concerned— grandparents, parents, stepparents, and children. The acceptance of new types of American families as viable and productive family forms is essential. We are faced with a new reality—the family scene of *Our Town* has changed.

NECESSARY TASKS IN THE ACHIEVEMENT OF STEPFAMILY INTEGRATION

Mourning the Losses Involved

Projections from demographic data indicate that 45% of the children born today in American will live in single-parent or stepparent house-holds before they reach the age of 18. By 1990 there will be more such households than biological family households.

These figures translate to large amounts of loss and pain—the main ingredients of the emotional context in which stepfamilies are born. In-complete mourning of past relationships can interfere with efforts to create a successful new stepfamily. All too often, children have not been allowed to acknowledge and experience the pain of their losses. Often during the single-parent phase, whether it follows a death or a divorce, when children have taken on responsibility for comforting and supporting a parent, their own hurt may go unnoticed. Anger and deviant behavior of the children may result, which often produces further loss rather than the support needed by the parent.

At the time of a remarriage, the adults may be on a pink cloud of rosy expectations. They believe that the children will welcome the wonderful new person entering their lives. From a child's point of view, however, the picture may look very different. Now the children must share their parent with another adult and perhaps with other children. They wonder how often they will see their other biological parent. They may be deeply concerned about whether there will be a place for them in the new household unit. Teenagers may be asked to give up their role as man of the house or father's helper and return to being a child again.

One such situation involved a stepmother who came bursting into the family in which her new husband had lived with his 16-year-old daughter. The teenager had cooked and kept house for her father for 2 years following her mother's death. Her new stepmother wanted to take charge, pushing her out of the kitchen. The sense of loss she experienced was so acute that the teenager tried to come between the new couple to regain her former status and position in the household.

There are also less easily recognized losses—the dream of what the former marriage was going to be even for the spouse who had finally been the one to want the divorce, or the lifelong expectations of what marriage would be like for a person not previously married who was marrying a person with children. The task of letting go of these dreams and fantasies is so difficult that many go through times of anger, then sorrow, before accepting reality.

Grandparents also have losses. The dreams they have dreamed for their children and for their family continuity and psychological sense of immortality have been shaken. They need time to mourn, to accept, and to move ahead to new commitments and relationships with new adults, stepgrandchildren, and a different family kinship network.

The Development of New Traditions

A newborn baby arrives with no expectations of what this world will be like. In a functional family, the parents manage to combine their own family traditions and ways of doing things into standard operating procedures for their household. They then start the process of parenting and adjusting as they interact with their growing child. At each stage of the child's life, negotiation and changes take place. There is nurturing and then limit setting as the child grows and explores the world. Family traditions are worked out. Halloween is a time for making candied apples; summer vacations at the beach become part of the life of the family.

For stepfamilies, limit setting has previously been added to nurturance. Each individual has definite ideas on how holidays are celebrated. Because ideas on discipline differ, both children and adults hold tightly to the familiar customs of their former households. Unfortunately, instead of adjustment, the adults are bewildered when their attempts to settle quickly into a family routine become dismal failures. A 15-year-old girl talking about her new stepfamily said,

I'm very sentimental, and I used to make flowery birthday cards and Christmas cards for everyone in the family. We had big parties on birthdays, and on Christmas Eve we sat up late and sang carols together. Now we get presents, but no birthday parties, and we go to bed early on Christmas Eve so that Mom and my stepdad can decorate the Christmas tree and put special presents in our stockings by the fireplace. It isn't the way it used to be, and it makes me feel that what we did before was wrong.

Negotiation is necessary in all families, but it is particularly important and difficult in stepfamilies in which there are no longer givens, even for the children, since they, too, have experienced other ways of living together. Obviously, house rules are necessary, but high-profile stepparents who enter with the idea of saving the family and wiping away the hurts of the past usually run into difficulty. A single-parent mother, for example, even though she has longed for someone to share the limit setting or discipline with her, often becomes fiercely protective of her children if her new husband is strict or disciplines differently than she had hoped. The children respond negatively because of their need to form a relationship before accepting active disciplining.

Family meetings during which feelings are accepted and ideas negotiated can be most helpful in evolving a new set of regulations and traditions for a new household. Often, combining traditions from the past by arranging special presents as well as a party on birthdays may ease the transition and convey the message that there is not a right or a wrong way of doing things—merely different ways. The traditions of today become the happy memories of the future.

The need to work together creatively toward effective solutions is not confined to the beginning months of the remarriage. Initially, there seems to be constant negotiation, but through the years new traditions must be worked out as family occasions arise. One young woman, marrying for the first time, was surprised when she purchased an up-to-date book on weddings only to find that it answered few of her questions because it was filled with ways of planning weddings with more than a single set of parents and two sets of grandparents. Many creative solutions can be found to most problems if the problems are approached with a willingness to consider different options.

Forming New Interpersonal Relationships

In a nuclear family the couple has the opportunity to solidify their relationship before children are added. This is not the case in a stepfamily, in which the new couple may be attempting to have a honeymoon in the middle of a crowd. Also, there are parent–child relationships of longer duration than the relationship of the new couple. Frequently, children are dropped on the doorstep of a remarried couple who have not planned to include them in their new household. Everyone may feel uneasy and trapped. The parent of the newcomers (whether their arrival was planned or not) may feel guilty at the unhappiness displayed on all sides and may push for quick stepparent–stepchild relationships, increasing the tension. There may be guilt, anger, and frustration, often followed by rejection and a sense of alienation. This can be particularly devastating for the stepfamily unit if the dissension interferes with the couple relationship.

Forty percent of second marriages end in divorce in the first 4 years, with children from a previous marriage increasing the likelihood of another divorce (Becker, Landes, & Michael, 1977). In families, the relationship of the couple is important for family functioning (Lewis, Beavers, Gossett, & Phillips, 1976). Couples in stepfamilies have many conflicting forces that can weaken their relationship:

- guilt at forming a new adult–adult relationship because it seems to be a betrayal of their earlier parent–child relationships,
- divisive behavior of children who may still retain the fantasy of getting their biological parents back together again,
- nonacceptance of the new partner and children by stepgrandparents or other close relatives, and
- neglect of the needs of stepfamilies by many institutions such as the schools, churches, and legal codes.

These internal and external stresses for remarried couples require that they make time to nourish their relationship, remaining conscious that sustaining a commitment to one another will serve to stabilize the new household unit. Such a commitment also acts as a model for the children as they grow up and separate from the family, establishing their own adult relationships.

Often stepgrandparents can be important figures in helping the formation of new relationships. Children are already accustomed to having more than one set of grandparents, so one or two more sets do not seem that unusual. Getting to know another branch of the family can assist stepparents and stepchildren in forming relationships with each other.

It is often difficult for parents to stand back and let stepparents and stepchildren do things together that will help build their relationship. This is particularly difficult if the remarried parent was unmarried for more than 2 or 3 years, making the bond between the parent and child very tight. A parent in this situation can have a strong internal conflict between wanting the steprelationships to be strengthened and, at the same time, feeling a loss in the closeness of the previous ties. For successful integration of the stepfamily, however, it is vitally necessary for new patterns to emerge.

Relationships between stepsiblings can also be important sources of richness and growth. Two stepbrothers in their early 20s, looking back on their 10 years of being together, spoke of their conscious effort to be friends and to learn from each other. As one said,

> I would never have chosen Charlie as a friend because we're so different, but I'm so pleased we took a chance and decided to try to make our new relationship work. I've grown and learned different kinds of things from him than I would have from my friends who were much more like me.

Relationships with the Other Biological Parent

Whether the other biological parent has died or is alive and well, living just across town, this person exerts a powerful influence on the stepfamily household. A parent who has died often gains a halo, which is hard to dislodge. A living parent often grows horns.

Too often, stepparents and their children move into the home previously lived in by the other adult and his or her children. In such situations, it is particularly difficult to feel like an insider who belongs there. When the former spouse has died, the house can seem haunted by a ghost. Even when this is not the case, there can still be territorial disputes. In a deep psychological sense, not letting go of the original home may indicate a failure to separate from the past relationship. It may signal sadness and incomplete mourning, or anger and bitterness.

Even when stepfamilies start out in a new home, there may be loyalty conflicts for the children, as well as for the remarried parent who feels caught between children, stepchildren, spouse, and ex-spouse. Many times, parents and new in-laws complicate matters further.

There are many different types of stepfamilies: those in which both new spouses have children or the stepparent has no children; those in which there has been a death or a divorce; or those in which the children are in the household most or all of the time or the children are seldom in the household. Although there are some elements common to all types of stepfamilies, there are differences as well. When a previously unmarried woman marries a man with custody of children or with children who spend every other week with them, the household has less balance than when both adults have been previously married and have children. In the former household, the single woman may feel alone in enemy territory, especially when she has moved away from her family and friends into her husband's neighborhood and life; in the latter, there may be more confusion and more new relationships and traditions to work out. If one of the biological parents has not remarried, developing or maintaining a working relationship among all the parental figures with regard to the children may be particularly difficult.

Sharing children stirs deep feelings of insecurity as well as sadness and loss. "Will Johnnie's stepfather do a better job of parenting than I did or than I can do now that I see him so little?" "Am I as good a mother as Jane? I have to do all the work and she has all the fun times with the kids 'cause they're only there on weekends."

Noncustodial parents feel particularly helpless, though often both parents have a sense of loss of control. They may attempt to gain mastery by attempting to control the ex-spouse rather than by attempting to control what is within their own sphere of power. When anger and bitterness result, the children may feel involved and responsible; their pain may be great and the burden so heavy that they feel compelled to choose sides. When the children become pawns in this way in the struggle between the adults, everyone loses.

Because of these struggles, biological parents often feel that they are helping themselves and their children if they quietly disappear, particularly if a stepparent is willing to take over. Research indicates, however, that such a withdrawal does not benefit the children (Wallerstein & Kelly, 1980). While they may have gained another important parental figure, they do not want to lose a primary relationship of great importance to their sense of personal worth and identity.

If at all possible, with the exception of situations of abuse or psychological breakdown, it is better for children to have contact—even though minimal—with both of their biological parents (Wallerstein & Kelly, 1980). If these adults, as well as the grandparents and stepparents, can accept each other's parenting skills and the children's needs for contact, stepfamily integration will be easier and smoother. The children, free to relate to all of the adults in their lives, do not have to take sides. Their different needs will be met by a larger number of caring adults

Satisfactory Movement between Households

Children are frequently members of at least two households with different rules, regulations, traditions, and ways of doing things. When these differences as viewed by the adults are respected as differences rather than there being one right household (one's own, naturally) and one wrong household (the other one, of course), the children can usually accept and adapt as long as the expectations in each household are clear to them. The adults need an inner security and a willingness to tolerate ambiguity for this to materialize. To illustrate, one stepmother had finally reached the end of her tolerance. Instead of once again repressing her feelings of anguish and insecurity she responded to her stepdaughter's complaint, "That's not the way my mother cooks noodles," by answering, "I guess that's right. I'm not your mother. She does things her way and I do them my way, but I am the resident mother in this house." Not unexpectedly, that was the end of similar complaints from the stepdaughter, since she could no longer play one person (or one household) against the other.

There are situations in which a parent has to act because the behavior in the other household is damaging to the children, but most complaints about the former spouse stem from fear and insecurity rather than from actual harm that is being done to the children, either psychologically or physically.

Although it appears paradoxical, there need to be clear household boundaries before there can be cooperation between the household members and psychological space for the children to move back and forth easily. A remarried father with custody of his two children panicked when his ex-wife returned to the area in which he and his new wife and children lived. He sought help, asking at the beginning of the first appointment, "Do I need to telephone my ex-wife and let her know everything we're going to be doing with the children?" This question expressed his confusion about where the boundaries should be. When his ex-wife came to pick up the children for a visit, she walked into his new home, used the telephone without asking, and roamed through the house at will. There were battles between the adults, and bitterness and upset feelings in the children, until household boundaries comfortable to the adults could be established. Only then could the new couple feel a sufficient sense of mastery to stop fighting each other and the husband's ex-wife. Then they were able to respect the needs of the children, allowing them freedom to move back and forth between their two households.

Having two different household units can be confusing and can lead to less predictability for both adults and children, but when children feel wanted in both households and comfortable in enjoying what each has to offer, there is a richness of experience and a variety of relationships for the children to take advantage of as they develop into adulthood. An 11-year-old boy, who spent Mondays and Wednesdays with his father and stepmother, Tuesdays and Thursdays with his mother, and alternate weekends in the two homes, told of his pleasure at this arrangement. He quickly acknowledged, however, that he would not want to go to a ballgame or to the zoo with all three adults together because "my Mom and Dad might start to argue." It seems that the adults rather than the children have the greatest difficulty accepting a family pattern in which children go back and forth between households.

The Effect of Two Households on Teenagers

While teenagers in all families are individuating and separating from their family, their peer group is very important to them. When a remarriage takes place and there are teenage children, parents and stepparents often interpret usual teenage behavior as an expression of belonging to the stepfamily rather than merely as the developmental stage of the young person. Often, however, teenagers are not motivated to become cooperative family members in a new family unit when they are already in the process of separating. When parents and stepparents attempt to force them to participate in the new family, active resistance occurs. As in all types of families, it may not be until the teenagers are grown up and independent that they will feel comfortable in returning to relate as individual young adults to their parents and stepparents.

With the birth of a child to the new couple, younger children, often becoming excited, begin to relate more closely to the stepfamily unit and to their stepparents. Teenagers, on the other hand, are often embarrassed and upset by such an event, particularly at first.

It is during the teen years that the teenagers are experiencing their own emerging sexuality. Stepfamilies are more stimulating places sexually for the teenagers than biological families. In biological families, children often consider their parents as nonsexual beings. Indeed, antagonisms between teenage stepsiblings and stepparents may sometimes erupt, masking the sexual attractions that are being experienced. One young adult expressed the conflicts well as he looked back to his teenage years in a stepfamily:

> I was always thinking about girls, and I was always thinking about sex. And one of my fantasy objects was my stepsister. This was particularly tough because I felt both attracted to women and afraid of women, and there she was in various states of undress. Whether she actually was or not, I really don't remember. I was attracted to her, and I was curious about her both as an individual and as a symbol. She was too close to ignore. I couldn't distance from her in that house.
>
> Another one of my objects was my stepmother. And that was even worse! It was even more threatening to me because I was attracted to her sexually, and I went out to her emotionally, too. There was a lot there in my head. Really my fear about my sexual feelings about my stepmother kept me from expressing some of my positive emotions towards her. (Visher & Visher, 1979, p. 177)

SUPPORT FOR STEPFAMILIES

Although over 500,000 new stepfamilies are being formed each year in the United States, it is only in recent years that this type of family has received attention. We believe that the major difficulty for individuals in many stepfamilies lies in the expectation that this type of family is the same as a biological or nuclear family. This belief, pervasive in our society, leads to unrealistic and unattainable expectations and goals that result in pain and stress for those involved. As in nuclear families, children in stepfamilies go through similar developmental stages, sibling rivalry exists, and couples need to work out their own intimacy issues. Unlike biological families, stepfamilies are born of many important losses and contain individuals who have not grown up together and established family rules and traditions. Stepparents and stepchildren may not even know each other's past nor recognize the meaning of a lifted eyebrow or the shrug of a shoulder. The steprelationships between stepsiblings and different generations have to be slowly forged between people who might never have chosen to relate to one another.

Stepfamilies, complex within their own family unit, are further complicated because there is an outside biological parent with whom the children need contact. Therefore, the household boundaries are permeable as the children move back and forth. Transition and change are constant and normal.

Because of the complicated situations that arise and the strength of the feelings that surface, individuals in stepfamilies often feel that there must be something very wrong with them. If they have experienced a previous marriage or marriages that did not work out, their lingering sense of failure often adds still another emotional load, so that competent and capable individuals find themselves unable to cope.

General patterns emerge:

- Stepmothers feel ignored and unappreciated by their stepchildren.
- Tensions are created between husband and wife as the husband feels guilty and upset that things are not going more smoothly.
- Stepfathers feel inadequate and impotent when their stepchildren pay little attention to them.
- Wives become critical and upset at their husband's attempts to gain some control.
- Children feel sad, helpless, and angry, fearing that they will have no secure place in the new household.
- Children fear that they will lose contact with parents and grandparents.

The task, then, is to chart the stepfamily territory so that the way becomes recognizable and familiar. Rearing children is not easy in any household. Maintaining a good couple relationship takes work; such relationships do not survive neglect and lack of awareness. Information, education, and support become especially important because there are special challenges and complexities and few models for individuals in stepfamilies. It is crucial to replace the old fantasy of family with acceptance of new family forms. When this happens, living in a stepfamily can become rewarding and deeply satisfying.

There is help for the couple whose story appeared at the beginning of this article. Therapists and counselors are struggling to understand the dynamics of stepfamilies; individuals and agencies are offering special courses and groups for stepfamilies; schools, churches, and the legal system are becoming sensitive to and working on the issues; and groups of stepparents are getting together to support and teach each other. A national organization, Stepfamily Association of America (900 Welch Road, Suite 400, Palo Alto, CA 94304), publishes a quarterly newsletter, *Stepfamily Bulletin,* for anyone interested in steprelationships. The Association also sends book lists and reprints to its members, provides training workshops for professionals, assists chapters and state divisions to form mutual support networks, and is engaged in community public education.

Stepfamilies and professionals who work with them need to know that their family complexity can bring richness and diversity to their members. Building new relationships makes stepfamily members sensitive to the importance of communication and emotional touching. Stepfamily members can experience the deep satisfaction and bonding that result from working together to meet difficult challenges. Learning to cope effectively with the pain of loss can produce an ability to deal creatively with the inevitable changes and losses that are a part of life itself.

REFERENCES

Becker, G.S., Landes, E.M., & Michael, R.T. An economic analysis of marital instability. *Journal of Political Economy,* 1977, *85,* 1141–1187.

Lewis, J.M., Beavers, W.R., Gossett, J.T., & Phillips, V.A. *No single thread: Psychological health in family systems.* New York: Brunner/Mazel, 1976.

Visher, E.B., & Visher J.S. *Stepfamilies: A guide to working with stepparents and stepchildren.* New York: Brunner/Mazel, 1979.

Wallerstein, J.S., & Kelly, J.B. *Surviving the breakup: How children and parents cope with divorce.* New York: Basic Books, 1980.

9. Facilitating Family Restructuring and Relinkage*

*Work on this article was supported by a grant to the Families of Divorce Project at the Philadelphia Child Guidance Clinic by the Pew Memorial Trust. The author would like to thank Braulio Montalvo for his helpful comments on the manuscript.

Marla Beth Isaacs, Ph.D.
Families of Divorce Project
Philadelphia Child Guidance Clinic
Philadelphia, Pennsylvania

Nine

Emily (age 8): I don't think I'll ever get used to it! (referring to mother kissing boyfriend)

Mother: Do you know why it bothers you?

Emily: I just wouldn't want another father, like I told you before.

Mother: But even if I got married again, whoever I marry would be my husband, but not your father, maybe your friend. Daddy would always be your father, always, no matter what.

Emily: Wouldn't he be my part father?

Susan (age 10): He'd be our stepfather.

Mother: Yeah.

Therapist: What's a stepfather?

Susan: Someone who's not really your father. Somebody who marries your mother.

AT SOME POINT IN THE DIVORCE PROCESS, ONE OR both parents become involved in a new relationship. It is the hope of the parents in such a relationship that the children will accept and like the new person. In some families, this occurs with little trouble. In other families the children's linkage to the new person is thwarted from the start. It is estimated that 20%–30% of all children will be affected by divorce. Out of these, 15%–20% will live in reconstituted or blended families (Furstenberg, 1979). These children number in the millions, and the problems facing them are not trivial.

Though all disruptions to family life share certain elements, the focus here is on families of divorce. For purposes of this article the definition of the divorce process is not bound by legal concepts. It could be that some people effectively divorce before legal action is completed, while some have not divorced even after. The finality of legal proceedings does not necessarily mark the end of the divorce process. Its end, rather, is marked when the participants have completed all emotional and interpersonal tasks in relation to the former partner and have rearranged that relationship so that they remain married as parents, not as spouses. New boundaries exist and the participants are anchored in a new life.

A blended family has been defined as one in which at least one partner of the new couple has had children from a previous union. For present purposes, however, marriage alone is not considered the factor that creates a blended family. In fact, a couple with children can marry with little actual blending taking place. A blended family is one in which two major tasks have been accomplished: (a) The new partners have accepted each other as executives in the new family hierarchy, and (b) the children have accepted the new partner without experiencing many problems of turf from unclear or dysfunctional boundaries.

In general, blending occurs as an almost invisible process involving intermediate steps toward the major tasks. These steps can be taken by the family early in the new relationship before marriage or even talk of marriage takes place. What is involved is a renegotiation of boundaries within the subsystem of the new unit —parent, new partner, and child— as well as within the larger family unit that includes the former spouse (the child's other parent). The way this process unfolds can either facilitate or impede blending.

In broad outline, when the steps in the process are taken correctly, they are often without consequence, and parents may not even have realized they have traversed a stage. Children have to deal with the space left by the parent now absent from the house. Many parents will naturally protect that space for the child rather than try to put in an understudy too quickly. Often the adversarial relationships experienced between a parent's new relationship and the ex-spouse are naturally circumvented. Families also see to it that the slight reversals of hierarchy occurring within the new family constellation are not chronic or taxing.

Many families complete the tasks successfully and move on, not receiving the formal help of mental health professionals. Other families get stuck, and blending is hampered.

PROBLEMS IN THE BLENDING PROCESS

When families are stuck, problems in the process of blending can be characterized by the three following situations:

1. A family acts like an instant family.
   (A) The space of the absent parent is invaded.
   (B) Forced blending occurs.
   (C) The new woman takes over parental function for father.
2. An adversarial relationship between the new partner and the child's other parent is established.
3. The family hierarchy is reversed, with the new partner lower on the hierarchy than the child.

These different situations reflect problems in the organization and maintenance of boundaries—with boundaries becoming either too weak, too rigid, or inappropriately placed.

Because the problems of blending are those of boundaries and structure, therapy is concerned with turf. Therefore, the significance of order and protocol in working with families must be emphasized. In practice, this means that although a therapist must consider the entire system and often work with it as well, the children of new partners cannot be brought into treatment without gaining the consent of the other parent. This is especially true when the noncustodial parent, who may not have been the one to bring the child to treatment, wishes to bring his or her new relationship to the therapy sessions with the children. The dynamics of consent are crucial. Once permission is obtained for participation in therapy, that permission needs to be clearly conveyed to the children. Only then can the children feel free to develop their relationship with the new partner, without worrying that such an effort is an act of disloyalty to their natural parent.

Obtaining consent can be problematic. For example, often the therapist is not asked, but a parent instead brings a partner to the therapy session—and sometimes to the first therapy session. When that occurs, the therapist has to tread a careful line. To see the new person can mean to sabotage the therapy for the other parent and, therefore, for the child, particularly if the relationship between the parents is a hostile or hurt one. To refuse to see the new person may mean insulting the parent who brought him or her, creating from the start the feeling that the therapist is on the side of the other parent. In such instances the therapist may have to meet the new partner in the waiting room or even bring the partner into the treatment room for the first few minutes and, after the greeting, define the immediate issues as having to do with the parent alone. It must be conveyed to the couple, however, that the new person is considered to be a valuable resource by the therapist, but the time for participation will be in later sessions. With such an approach, the new partner is also less likely to sabotage what goes on in the treatment and to be threatened by the parent's participation in therapy. The therapist then has the time to gain consent from the other parent for the eventual participation of the former spouse's new partner.

PROCESSES AND THERAPEUTICS: CASE VIGNETTES

The Instant Family

Blending takes place through the gradual rearrangement of the structure of the family. Families become instant families when an adult's presumption is that the individuals involved do not have to go through any process to become a new family. This occurs for varied reasons and cannot be predicted from the character of the participants alone. For some, this inability to experience the transition as a process may reflect an underlying wish of a parent that the problems they have created for themselves and for their children would simply vanish. For others, who are more than just imposers, it can still be narcissism or even naiveté that prevents them from seeing that the child has to do his or her own working through of the divorce and integration with the new partner. These adults may have successfully moved through the stages of their own disengagement from their spouse and reengagement to the new person, but do not realize that their children have to effect their own adjustment to the divorce. Other people may strive to become instant families as a way to continue a fight with the ex-spouse; others may do it to try to finalize the end of the previous marriage.

Three types of processes are often found in instant families. The first is the invasion of the space of the absent parent. Families often evolve special rituals between parents and children. These rituals are often small and concrete—a goodnight story from dad told in a certain chair or making a special recipe with mom—things that might never have been talked about, yet represent for the child the stability of the relationship.

When such rituals are not reserved for the absent parent but are handed over to the new person, the space of the absent parent has been invaded.

Forced blending, a more extreme process, occurs when the parent and the new partner form an abstract concept of how the family ought to operate and then impose their ideas on the children. A rule might be that "children must always be loyal to the original parent" or that "children will always accept the new partner as parent." Whatever the rules and assumptions of the new family unit, the situation is interpreted as forced blending when the parent and new partner impose these ideas on their children. Blending cannot be based on a formula.

A third process found in the instant family involves the issue of replaceability of dominant parental roles. The case in which father's new woman takes over his parental functions early, allowing him to retreat to a more familiar and more comfortable role of secondary caretaker, happens often. With this arrangement a structure is imposed on the children that is likely to create hostility and, in the end, hamper the family's ability to blend. Case vignettes illustrating these three processes follow.

Invading the Space of the Absent Parent

Mother to 8-year-old:	You said something to me when I was giving Harvey a backrub in the living room. Do you remember what that was that you said?
8-year-old:	I remember, but it would be weird to say except in front of any of my relatives.
Mother:	Is it OK if I tell Dr. I?
8-year-old:	I suppose.
Therapist:	Wait a minute, can I be considered a relative for tonight?
8-year-old:	Yeah, I said, "Don't get personal on the couch."
Therapist to girl:	Why did that bother you? Can you tell your mother?
8-year-old:	Because you used to do that to Daddy.

The dilemma posed for this child involved a violation of the space that belonged to the parent. This child had often seen her mother during the marriage give backrubs to her father in that same spot, on the living room couch. She was able, in fact, to tolerate behavior of a more intimate nature between her mother and her mother's new man, but the history of this particular action made the backrub intolerable for her to watch. The concreteness of children's thinking has to be respected. "Don't get personal on the couch" means just that. For this child, on the couch or not a backrub may not have been all right.

A parent must protect the turf of the other parent from intrusions of a new relationship. In their anxiety, parents often push the new partner into the absent parent's role, thereby rushing a process that, by definition, takes time. The job of the therapist, then, is to emphasize to the parent the importance of protecting that space. In the case vignette presented, the therapist advised the mother to stop the backrubs because at this time her daughter could not tolerate them. The therapist then worked out with the mother a more appropriate public pacing of her relationship in front of her children.

In contrast to traditional structural views that presume that if a parent is comfortable the child will be also, this is not the case in divorce and relinking situations. Rather, children have their own existence—and children have to effect their own adjustment to the divorce. It is important to listen to the child who cannot tolerate watching the backrub or the kissing between mother and boyfriend. A child who challenges the mother never to kiss her man is a child in charge, which is a different situation than that being presented here. A therapist and parent must watch for what is bearable for the child and must treat the child with respect. Health depends on parental acknowledgment that the child is part of the system and that what parents do is not strictly up to the parents. They must watch the children.

To facilitate a relationship between the child and the new partner, it is paramount that the parent protect the space of the absent parent. That space might be a particular game that the absent parent and the child always played together, the reading of a particular bedtime story, the process of going to church as a family, or even the backrub that the child used to witness the absent parent receiving on the living room couch. If the new partner is respectful of that space and does not enter until invited by the child, the possibilities of linkage are enhanced.

Forced Blending

A mother who has two daughters, 5-year-old Amy and 9-year-old Deborah, remarries. The children see their biological father weekly, but the mother informs her daughters that her new husband is also to be their new father, and they are to call him dad. The new man, who was loving towards the children, was happy to be elevated to this role all the more because he has stopped visiting his own two daughters who lived with his first wife on the opposite coast. A year and a half into the marriage, this family came to treatment after the younger child had become hyperactive in kindergarten and the mother had discovered the diary of the older child in which she wrote about her unhappiness.

The mother's directive had had a differential impact on her daughters. Nine-year-old Deborah complained when alone with the therapist that she could not stand to call her stepfather dad. She said that he could never be her father, that she already had a father, but that she was afraid that if she called him anything else she would get in trouble with her mother. Five-year-old Amy, who had been just $2^1/2$ years old when the marriage ended, felt as if her stepfather were her real father and was comfortable calling him dad. However, if during visitation with her real father, she accidently referred to her stepfather as dad, her real father would become furious and would order her never to call him that.

The older girl, then, experienced an invasion of father's turf in the mother's directive to call the new man something that could only be used for her biological father. The younger also experienced an invasion of turf, only reversed. She had grown to love this new man who acted like her father. Thus she became confused and guilty each time her biological father became angry at her for referring to her stepfather in the only way that was natural for her. By forcing the blending in the way that she did, the mother had invaded what was father's space for her 9-year-old. By not allowing the younger child to call stepfather dad, the biological father was not respecting and protecting the space that had been built between the 5-year-old and the mother's new husband. Each parent operated under an abstract conception of how children in a family ought to feel and tried to impose their rules on their children.

The therapeutic task with forced blending becomes one of boundary respecting. In this family, the directive to call the stepfather dad had to be removed. The therapist told the mother and her husband that by forcing the issue of calling her stepfather dad onto the older daughter, they ran the risk of preventing the emergence of any true closeness between the two of them. Simultaneously, it was important to emphasize throughout that the new husband was not just any other person to the children. He was accepted by the therapist as an important person and one whom the girls regarded as such. In a family session, he and the children were given the task of coming up with a special name for him, one that would connote the special place that he had in their lives. It became important for the mother to tell the children that they could call him anything they wished, but that she no longer required that they call him dad.

The therapeutic strategy with the biological father was similar but more difficult to achieve. He could not be left out of the therapeutic work, since he was clearly part of the system that was making the blending difficult for his children. The therapist joined with him, by agreeing that the children should not be required to call anyone but him dad, and that, in fact, his older daughter would probably never be comfortable calling anyone but him dad. He was reminded, however, that his younger daughter was only 2½ years old when he left the marriage and was told that it was appropriate for her age in a good relationship to naturally call stepfather dad. The work with the biological father involved helping him to understand that his younger daughter's ability to form intimate relationships despite the divorce was a sign of her adjustment and that that was a credit to him and a good prognosis for her future development. He had to allow her to call stepfather dad without making her feel badly about doing so.

In divorce counseling, the therapist can be alerted to the early stages of forced blending and can intervene so that the situation does not become a chronic one, as in the case just described. Forced blending usually implies an assumption on the part of the parent that his or her children will fully accept the new person, as quickly as the parent had, and in a special role. In one case seen in the Families of Divorce Project, a 10-year-old girl complained to the therapist about the mother's boyfriend: "She always tells us how much she loves him, and that makes us feel that we have to love him too. And we don't see him as much as she does." This mother was pushing her new man onto her children by not protecting them from her excitement about him in the early phases of the relationship.

Replaceability: A Mother Is a Mother Is a Mother

A 45-year-old father of an 11-year-old boy and a 15-year-old girl was living with a 30-year-old woman who had no children of her own. Five or six times a year, the children would visit him for a week or two at a time. The father, a doctor and a professor, had an inflexible schedule, but the woman was able to return home at 3:00 P.M. daily. During his children's visits, the father continued with his normal routine and even flew out of town on occasion to give talks. His young woman was given the role of caretaker, cook, and entertainer. After several such visits, the 11-year-old, who was having problems with his mother, came to live permanently with his father. However, at this time the father was even more unable to free up his schedule. His new partner, instead, gave up her social contacts to be home by 3:00 P.M. because she was worried about the boy's hanging out in the neighborhood. With very strict cleanliness standards she had also become the disciplinarian of the boy. The father and the boy were able to maintain a conflict-free relationship, but the tension was expressed in the new woman–boy dyad. The new partner felt overburdened, and the boy missed time with his father and resented the young woman's telling him what to do since she was not his mother.

Therapy with the family involved first helping the father to see what the effects of his abdication were on his son and on his new partner. This man had established a pattern of denial that protected him from seeing the extent to which his partner was burdened with the new task of mothering his son and how upset the boy was at seeing so very little of him. Breaking through his denial was accomplished when both his son and his partner began to tell him in the therapy sessions how they were feeling. The father then had to reset his priorities. He had hoped to form an instant family so that he could have his son, his work, and his woman, and he had thought that he had been managing successfully in all three areas. He was now forced to reexamine his commitments and to face, with his partner, the ways in which he was re-creating his first marriage by giving the full job of child care with its inherent headaches and problems to the woman. His pretending that everything was the same and that people were replaceable had been a denial that the divorce had created any trauma for his son, like simply changing clothing or putting on a different mask.

The Adversarial Relationship between New Friend and Other Parent

16-year-old:	(talking about mother's reaction to his visitation with father and his new woman) I wish she would just act like it was just Dad we were visiting. Like she wouldn't even mention anything about her and wouldn't ask us about her.
Therapist:	Do you think your mom could do that?
16-year-old:	No, it's like a birthmark, it just won't go away.

Eight months after the separation, the mother pumped her children after every visit with their father who was living with a woman. The children had asked her not to ask about the woman, but the mother said that if she did not ask, she would still be wondering about it. This mother never met her former husband's new partner, but her hostility toward the woman was felt constantly by her children.

The relationship between the new partner and the ex-spouse is often the most difficult one in which to intervene. Depending on how the marriage terminated, people often face periods of intense depression and loss of self-esteem. A natural target of anger and jealousy is the new partner of the ex-spouse, all the more so when this person is perceived as having contributed to the dissolution of the marriage, or when one parent had hoped that the marital relationship would not end. If an adversarial relationship develops and becomes chronic, it can have lasting effects on the children and on the relationship between the children and their parents. When loyalty battles become exacerbated, some children may feel the need to protect the parent who does not have a new relationship. Others might wish to be close to the new partner, but the hostility of one of their parents would make them feel guilty about this.

In the case described, the therapist was not trying to make allies out of the mother and the father's new woman. That goal would have been an absurd one given the intensity of the mother's feelings, her jealousy, and her hurt. The therapist was trying to keep the mother from involving her children in the adversarial relationship by providing a different outlet for her to talk about rather than the other woman. The outlet was the therapist herself. The therapist, additionally, had to help the mother see the effect that her pumping was having on the children and finally, how, if she kept it up, the children would blame her for cutting off their relationship with the woman who was living with their father.

Although in this instance there was only minimal success in extricating the children from the mother's wrath at the father's new partner, an ultimate goal is to alter the adversarial relationship between a parent and the other parent's new partner. Care must be taken in determining when to attempt to make allies out of adversaries, but, when successful, the children benefit considerably.

The Reversed Hierarchy

The father is engaged to a woman whom he plans to marry within the year. His 9-year-old daughter visits him on weekends, and during these visits, the father sleeps in the bed with his daughter and his fiancée leaves the apartment. When they are together in the car, the child wants to sit in the front seat with her father and his fiancée even though the car has bucket seats. The father allows this despite the fact that his fiancée has complained repeatedly that this makes her uncomfortable. The father described an incident in which the fiancée told the father's daughter that she could not sit around the living room with a wet head:

> Father: I can see the value in that, like drying her hair, I can see it. OK, her hair should be dried instead of sitting around on a chilly night with wet hair. But like even this weekend, we had a discussion about it and I said, "Hey, get off the kid's back. I really don't like the way you treat her."

The father, in a coalition with his daughter, places the child higher than his new woman in the family hierarchy. The result of this is that the child is disobedient to the fiancée and senses correctly that her father will support her. He is not treating his new woman like a wife—a poor prognostic sign for their marriage.

Therapy in this case centered around showing the father that the family hierarchy was a skewed one and supporting the fiancée's right instead of the child to be Number One with her man. This vignette was extracted from a more complete case study, presented next, in which techniques restructuring the family hierarchy will be more carefully reviewed.

FACILITATING RELINKAGE: A CASE STUDY

The following case study illustrates the above processes and their therapeutic handling as they occurred within the divorce therapy of a 9-year-old girl. The case illustrates how the therapist can work with the entire system to facilitate relinkage. For dydactic purposes, a unit consisting of four people was chosen. In one house lives the mother, who is the custodial parent, and Rachel, her 9-year-old daughter who was 6½ years old at the time of the separation. Rachel visits her father every other weekend. During the last year he has become involved with Lynn, a woman he plans to marry before the year is out. They do not live together, but in the last 6 months, Lynn has stayed at the father's home, with the exception of those nights when the child has been with her father. Sessions 11–13 in a 14-session therapy best illustrate key themes and issues that arise for children and adults in the relinkage process. The 11th session was with the father, the fiancée, and the child; the 12th was with the mother and the child; and the 13th was with the father and the fiancée.

For the 11th session, the father appeared with his fiancée, having given neither his daughter nor the therapist any advanced warning. He had on previous occasions brought up his desire to have Lynn accompany him on his visits, so the therapist had had time to explain this to the mother and clear it with her. The therapist respected protocol, so the three could be seen on that day, once the therapist clarified for the child that the mother knew and approved that Lynn would be coming to a session. The therapist then began this new phase of therapy by asking the father for a statement of the problem. He brought up three points: (a) His daughter had not accepted his divorce, nor that he plans to marry Lynn. (b) He feels torn between what he wants for himself in his new life with his wife-to-be and what he wants to have with and for his daughter. (c) Lynn has problems adjusting suddenly to having an instant family. Lynn countered that the major adjustment for Rachel was the fact that she had become deeply involved with Rachel's father before the child had adjusted to the fact that her parents were going to be divorced. In her opinion the child has not adjusted because her parents failed to adequately explain to her that their separation was to be a permanent one. She adds about the child:

> Lynn: I think that there's a lot of strong loyalty to her mother that she's afraid that she's going to have to give up because of me. Or that I might ask her or her father might ask her to have loyalties to me that she can't bring herself to have because she has them for her mother, which is the most natural thing.

Lynn is talking about boundaries and Rachel's fear of being asked to cross boundaries by instantly having a very special relationship to her father's wife-to-be. In the following dialogue with Lynn, the therapist helps Rachel to see that her dad's new partner does not have these expectations of her:

> Therapist: Do you think that Rachel could ever feel about you the way she feels about her mother?
> Lynn: No.
> Therapist: Do you think she should?
> Lynn: No.

It is at this point that Rachel listens to Lynn, the intruder who says, "I don't want to take over." It may appear as if this arrangement is a dyadic one, between Lynn and Rachel, but in fact it is a triangular arrangement. The father, through his passivity, has supported Lynn's taking over with the child, helping to foster these expectations in Rachel.

This therapeutic maneuver represents a protection of the space belonging to the mother.

The intruder continues:

> Lynn: I think she is not sure of what her role should be. I think that's the problem. So as a result I guess it's difficult to put another adult who's going to marry her father into perspective, like where does that person fit in my life?
>
> Therapist
> to Lynn: Where do you fit?
> Lynn: I don't know.
> Therapist: In Rachel's life.
> Lynn: I don't know.

The woman's uncertainty about where she fits in the child's life must also be understood as an expression of uncertainty about where she stands with the child's father. This kind of dialogue in the therapy helps the family work themselves out of the position of being an instant family. Talking about such issues is a direct statement that as a unit they are not yet a family, and therefore the assumptions that they are already blended, which have proven troublesome for all involved, begin to be dispelled. The therapist next establishes that the child is not the identified patient by turning to her and saying that if the grown-ups do not know where Lynn fits, she, a child, could not possibly know either. Finally, the therapist indicated that the father is the main person who must help to reorganize the family structure. Singling father out in this way takes some of the pressure off the fiancée and puts it where it belongs, with the parent of the child. Until now, Lynn has done all of the worrying and all of the father's work. Not only does this represent a re-creation of the father's previous marriage, in which his wife did all the work, but it places undo strain on the fiancée.

In working with families that are becoming blended, therapists must pay careful attention to problems of the couple that are detoured through the other spouse or through the child. Tension created by the presence of the child can lead to questions of loyalty and commitment within the adult relationship. Rather than deal directly with that difficult issue, people often choose to label the child as the trouble—and the other parent as the one who created that trouble—thus protecting themselves from looking at any conflict within the new relationship. When this happens, therapy must address this process. In the session presented here, Lynn felt supported by the therapist and began to talk about how she and the child's father have different expectations of Rachel. Rather than fully accuse her new man, however, Lynn found a ready target in his former spouse.

> Lynn: I think my major problem is I don't know what things are expected of her from her mother and I know what my expectations are, but her father lets a lot of things slide so he doesn't have the same kind of expectations that I do.
>
> Therapist: I think the major problem is not that you don't know what to expect from her mother but that you and her father don't agree on what is expected.

The therapy involves forcing the couple to examine their relationship. The therapist asks Lynn if her man will support her. Afraid to examine his nonsupport, she tries to detour the problem through her adversary. The true unknowns for this woman are what the father expects of his daughter and whether he will give her license to intervene in these areas with Rachel.

The therapist continues to focus on the couple's relationship:

> Therapist to couple: How are the two of you going to be able to get together on this?
>
> Therapist to Lynn: Because the way it's set up now, you get to be the bad guy.
>
> Lynn: Exactly. An example of me being the bad guy, my car has bucket seats, and Rachel always wants to sit in the front seat, and the way bucket seats go it's not comfortable for her to sit in the middle section between the two seats because the seat belts are there so she always has to sit in the front seat and what happens is she winds up sitting on my side and I'm

> squashed; she's comfortable and I'm squashed. . . .
> She says "Can I sit in the front seat?" and he says
> "Yeah, OK, sit in the front seat." I don't think that's
> something she should have a choice. . . . It's a mat-
> ter of three people; that car is not built for having
> three people sit in the front.

A car that fits two in the front is a beautiful metaphor to characterize the problems of this emerging family. The father chooses to make his new woman uncomfortable rather than his little girl and is trying to fashion a family with three people at the helm. He is not treating his woman like a wife and acts as though the car is a trivial issue. It is not trivial. Rather, it is part of the process of the new woman trying to find a place with her man and with his child. In doing so, however, the fiancée never gives the father an ultimatum, that either his child sits in the back or she will leave. She is not convinced that she has a right to make that kind of assertion, nor is she certain about how her man would react.

It is the therapist's role to strengthen the new woman's belief in her right to be next to her man. But the fiancée hesitates because she is afraid of failing, knowing that his previous wife similarly failed. She knows that in the previous marriage, the child came first. She asks the therapist if the child's mother is now able to tell her to sit in the back seat if that is where she ought to be. Hoping to make allies of Lynn and the mother, the therapist gives assurance that the mother would do just that.

In an effort to form an alliance between these two women, the therapist portrays them as facing the same problem and dilemma and maybe even sharing the same values. Each time Lynn tries to detour the problem by bringing up her lack of knowledge of what happens to the child when at home with the mother, the therapist provides information about that mysterious relationship in a way that portrays the two women as similar. By asserting that things are not that different at home with Rachel, the therapist circumvents an attempted detouring of the problem and removes the excuse offered for why the couple themselves cannot work together to alleviate the tension with the child. The therapist asserts that the father's and his fiancée's ability to agree on the demands to be made on Rachel is the main thing that will make the difference as to whether or not the child complies. The therapist is addressing the issue of hierarchy and of the adults being in charge and plans to pursue it further in a session alone with the two adults.

As this session draws to a close, the fiancée describes a way in which they have been acting as if they are already a family. She points out that almost immediately after they started to date, Rachel was with the two of them, curtailing any time alone that Rachel had with her father. She suggested that perhaps Rachel would like to have some time alone with her father. Though this is another instance of the new partner doing the work and worry for father, it is structurally a beneficial move, since the child begins to see Lynn as a potential ally. The child readily admitted that she had indeed missed time alone with her father; they then planned to reinstitute special time for the two of them. Thus, boundaries are beginning to be restored, the forced blending is interrupted, and the focus of the problem is moved from the child to the relationship between the two adults.

The Creation of a Helpful Foursome: Work with the Mother

The thrust of the next session was to begin to make allies out of adversaries. This is difficult to accomplish and will not succeed with many families. It was attempted here because the hostility between the two women was under control, and the mother no longer wanted an intimate relationship with her former spouse. The strategy of the therapist was to change certain key assumptions held by the mother that in turn would allow her to change her behavior toward her daughter as well as toward her ex-spouse's new partner. The assumptions that the therapist created were as follows:

1. **It is helpful to the mother and to Rachel if dad's fiancée is involved with Rachel.** The therapist created this assumption through a series of questions about the mother's former spouse. The therapist asked the mother if her former husband is the kind of man who knows how to take care of a little girl. Would he notice if she was sitting around with a wet head in a cold room? Does he know how to braid her hair so that it looks just right? Will he know to send her to bed at the right time? The mother knew that her former husband was not that kind of person, and she began to see that her daughter would be better cared for if his new woman were doing some of the nurturing.

2. **It is a bad reflection on the mother when Rachel disobeys dad's fiancée.** Using the same strategy as used earlier with the fiancée, now the therapist portrays the fiancée as having similar values to mother. The therapist then characterizes Rachel's disrespectful behavior as

behavior the mother would not approve of and tells the mother that dad's fiancée is beginning to think that mother is a pushover because she must allow this kind of behavior at home. The mother then sees that her daughter's behavior is creating an offensive image of what mother is like at home. This is an appeal to the mother's pride. The key is that mother is proud of her competence as a mother, and her pride takes ascendance over any conflict about her daughter's liking dad's fiancée.

3. **It is the mother's problem that Rachel does not accept the finality of the separation.** In this case the mother knows that her daughter does not accept the finality of their separation. She told the therapist that Rachel "sees me as his wife, divorced or not, and she knows that there's a divorce and that it's final and everything is over with but in the back of her mind she still sees me as married to him." The therapist tells the mother that this will create a real problem for mother when mother wants to start dating.

> Therapist: Are you going to get it from her, if you start dating with her having these ideas! And why should you get the blame for being the one to break up the marriage?
> Mother: I don't get blamed.
> Therapist: You will if you start dating.
> Mother: Do you think so?
> Therapist: Yes.
> Mother: Terrific!
> Therapist: Why should you get the flak? You see, what Rachel sees is that you're Number 1 for her father, because that Number 1 place is being saved for mom and Rachel is kind of house sitting in that place, like when she sleeps with dad, it's like your ghost is there. . . . I mean why should she believe that it's over when she knows about intimacies that adults share in long-term relationships and she sees that dad is somehow saving the Number 1 spot next to him not for this woman he is going to marry. She sees that dad keeps his new lady out in the car when he comes to pick Rachel up. This is a real set up for you. If you start dating, you'll be the one she'll see as breaking the marriage up. Rachel sees reality so

she knows that when dad picks her up, he has Number 1 lady in the house so he can't bring Number 2 in, he has to keep her out in the car. Quite a stunt they're pulling on you and it's not doing you a favor actually.

The therapist does not center on changing the daughter. Rather, the therapist centers on the dangers that the child's behavior will create for mother. This motivation through enlightened self-interest is effective with certain kinds of participants and, in this case, helped the mother to see that it is to mother's advantage to accept responsibility for the child's nonacceptance of the divorce and then to work on it.

4. **The mother contributes to Rachel's reluctance to accept the finality of the separation.** The mother is confronted with the situation that she has perpetuated with Rachel's negative feelings toward the breakup of her parents, and that she will have to pay the price for this when she starts to date. The therapist then brings up the fact that in 2 years the mother has not dated and suggests that Rachel must have the idea that the mother still does care about her ex-husband, and that mother does not want him to be with another woman. Part of divorce therapy is to help the adults to move ahead with their own lives. By dealing with her daughter's unwillingness to relinquish the marriage, the mother was working indirectly on her own feelings about ending that part of her life and moving on. The therapist helps this process by asking mother if she can tolerate no longer being her husband's wife. Does the mother want her little girl to continue to protect that place of hers next to her former husband? The mother was able to answer a clear "no" to both these questions. The therapist then tells the mother that her daughter is not aware of how she really feels about her ex-spouse because why else would the mother not talk to the fiancée when she comes to the house with dad—and why would the mother never allow Lynn in the house?

Behavior Change

The mother is now ready to begin to change her behavior. She asks the therapist if she ought to talk with dad's fiancée in front of Rachel; she is not ready yet to have her in the house. The therapist then brings the child into the interview room. They talk about what happens during visitation:

> Therapist: Maybe Rachel has the idea that you don't really want her to listen to Lynn.
> Mother: Well, she has the wrong idea. When you are over at daddy's house and Lynn tells you something to do, then she's the one you have to listen to.

The mother forcefully tells her daughter that she wants her to obey dad's fiancée. As the mother and her ex-spouse's fiancée move toward becoming allies, the goal is realized. The mother also begins to let go of her hold on her previous marriage and prepares to move ahead with her own life.

As mentioned previously, the 13th session was with dad and his fiancée. They report that Rachel acted differently during her last visit and that things had gone smoothly for the first time in a long while. They knew that they were there to deal with their own relationship. The therapist moved in to support the fiancée:

> Therapist: The two of you need to find ways to have Rachel realize that the Number 1 lady is sitting right there (pointing to Lynn).
> Therapist to Lynn: Right now she knows that you're the lady that her dad keeps out in the car.

Lynn admitted to not feeling very good about that arrangement, and dad was forced to confront his behavior, which was being called into question now by both the therapist and his fiancée. The therapist reminds them about their different expectations of Rachel and how the fiancée becomes the bad guy when she tells Rachel what to do. This is done to underline the crucial role that the father plays in facilitating the relationship among the three of them.

> Therapist to father: You have to do something so that Lynn doesn't feel that she's walking on egg shells—that every word has to be weighed that she says to Rachel. You're the only one who can change that.

> Father: By the same token, at some points I felt that every word I had to say to Rachel or to Lynn, to either of them in front of either of them, where I worried, oh, if I say this to Rachel, then Lynn will get upset, or to Lynn, then Rachel will get upset. Why does that have to be?

The father is clearly feeling the tension as well. It is his fiancée who underlines the change that has to take place—a change in the hierarchy.

> Lynn: I'm coming to a realization that if I'm his wife, I'm first. Now that's hard. And I'm first now. I can understand how it would really really hurt her. Because I think that Rachel knew that she was really first, above her mom when they were married. So all of a sudden, not is it only the relationship of mother and father breaking up, but somebody's usurping her place.

The fiancée has accepted the support and encouragement of the therapist and asserts her right to be the one in the front seat with her husband-to-be. She is not, however, entirely certain that she will not find herself in the same position as the first wife. She chooses to report an intimacy between the father and daughter that points to the coalition between them, their showering together, which he had stopped only when she complained. Hearing her doubt, the therapist brings up the father's tendency to let things slide and ends the session by fantasizing the worst alternative:

> Father: I think, why can't I let it all slide?
> Therapist: You can let it slide, but what you'll have is a spoiled brat and another divorce. That's what it would mean if you would really let all these things slide.

In these three sessions, the family unit made significant gains. The mother relinquished her hold on her old marriage and made her feelings clear to her daughter. The mother's space was protected for the child, and the forced blending was curtailed with an exploration of the dynamics of the new family, with special time set aside for father and child. The fiancée's fears of the reversed hierarchy, where she was less important than the child, were heard, and some suggested changes were made to correct it. Finally, inroads were made in creating allies out of the adversarial relationship that had been developing between the two women. The work that remained was work for the couple. The question that remained for the therapist was whether the father would indeed let things slide and thereby re-create his failed first marriage in his second marriage, or whether, with his fiancée's help, he would be able to allow her to sit beside him in the car, with the child in the back seat.

SUMMARY

This article focused on the processes that occur when families that are becoming blended get stuck. The blending process is hampered when the family acts like an instant family, the new partner and absent parent develop an adversarial relationship, and the hierarchy within the new family becomes skewed. Why is it important to understand these processes? First, with the prevalence of divorce in this country, many children find themselves experiencing the transition to a new family relationship. By looking at the failures the mental health profession can learn how to intervene. Second, these processes occur early; correcting them is preventive work. It is around early problems in blending that toxic attitudes toward the child get crystallized in the new partner. Early intervention provides a special opportunity for working with the family because the family is in a state of flux and is therefore more open to change. Third, early intervention can prevent a second divorce. Divorce can either be an enlightened, growth-producing move that can lead to a successful second marriage, or it can lead to a repetition of the first marriage. A goal of early intervention, then, is to prevent the replication of bad marriages.

REFERENCE

Furstenberg, F., Jr. Recycling the family: Perspectives for a neglected family form. *Marriage and Family Review*, 1979, 2 (3).

10. Use of Group Educational Techniques with Remarried Couples*

*This study was partially funded by a grant from the Kempner Foundation of Galveston, Texas, whose interest and support were greatly appreciated. The authors wish to extend their gratitude to Olga Antonetti and Gila Arnoni for their assistance with the research. In addition, appreciation is extended to John Ambler and Patrick Brady for reviewing the manuscript.

Carol Ann Brady, Ph.D.
Texas Research Institute of Mental Sciences
Houston, Texas

Joyce Ambler, M.S.W.
Texas Research Institute of Mental Sciences
Houston, Texas

Ten

THE PHENOMENON OF REMARRIAGE HAS CONTINUED TO increase, along with the better publicized, marked increase in divorce. This has led researchers to urge mental health professionals to broaden their view of acceptable family structures (Ahrons, 1981) and to develop a variety of skills for helping members of two previous families form a satisfactory new family unit (Ransom, Schlesinger, & Derdeyn, 1979; Sager, Walker, Brown, Crohn, & Rodstein, 1981).

The need to maintain continuity of parenting while simultaneously forming a new marital bond creates unique problems for the remarried couple. They must deal with a number of potential causes of stress: structural elements absent in the traditional nuclear family; the loss of a primary relationship by at least two family members; and, in the case of children, the absence of a biological parent. All of these stresses are exacerbated by the absence of an adequate framework to guide remarried couples toward a new family organization (Messinger & Walker, 1981; Sager et al., 1981). According to Walker and Messinger (1979), the boundaries of the reconstituted family are more permeable and the roles of family members are more ambiguous than in a nuclear family. Stepparents in particular often feel inadequately prepared to deal with issues involving discipline of stepchildren, communication with former spouses, and generally defining their role as stepparents. Apprehensiveness may lead to pseudomutuality, denial of problems, hostility, and idealization of the reconstituted family, all of which may further compound the couple's difficulty in addressing and resolving problems (Goldstein, 1974).

In an attempt to develop programs to assist remarried couples in forming new families, several authors have proposed the use of group educational models. Messinger (1976), for example, interviewed 70 couples involved in the formation of a stepfamily and examined ways in which the couples felt that their adjustment to the new marriage could have been facilitated. Parents stated that information on integrating the children into the family, handling finances, and similar issues would have been helpful. Messinger concluded that education to prepare couples for remarriage could reduce many potential problems. Messinger and Walker (1981) offered specific suggestions on topics for remarriage groups, including such issues as relationships with former spouses, financial arrangements, and perception of family members' roles and responsibilities in adjusting to the remarriage. Also, reported data from stepparents attending a 4-week discussion class on remarriage listed the following areas as most often mentioned among the participants: conflict involving discipline of stepchildren, being viewed as a bad guy by stepchildren, difficulties with former spouses, and poor marital communication (Visher & Visher, 1978).

In addition to discussion of issues important to stepparents, the supportive nature of the group can help remarried couples deal with other important problem areas, including lack of consolidation of the remarriage, incomplete mourning for the lost marital relationship, and guilt and conflict about the children (Sager et al., 1981). In reference to the value of groups in dealing with a sense of isolation common in stepfamilies, Jacobsen (1979) reported that group members in stepparent coping sessions expressed their anger and ambivalence openly and were surprised to discover that the feelings that they considered unusual were shared by others. Similarly, Mowatt (1972) stated that a group of stepfathers and their wives reported feelings of peer group acceptance and identification as a result of group participation. These results parallel conclusions that group techniques with other populations such as foster parents (Guerney & Wolfgang, 1981) and parents of newborn infants (Kagey, Vivace, & Lutz, 1981) are effective in reducing a sense of aloneness as well as increasing positive parenting skills.

The program reported here attempted to combine research with clinical service to stepparents. In terms of service, the program offered information about stepparenting issues. In reference to research, it was hypothesized that (a) stepparents would show a discrepancy between their evaluation of current family social climate and ideal family social climate; (b) stepparents involved in an educational group would report at the conclusion of the program less discrepancy between current and ideal perceptions of family social climate; and (c) stepparents involved in an educational group would show an increase in their understanding of stepparent issues as well as agreement with current information about stepfamilies.

METHOD

Subjects

Thirty-three remarried, middle-class, well-educated couples participated in the project. One wife and 2 husbands were dropped from the sample because they did not attend at least three of four sessions. Of the 32 wives and 31 husbands remaining, 3 missed one session, but the rest were present for all four sessions. The average age of the wives was 33.8 years, whereas the average for husbands was 36.8 years. Eighty percent had at least 2 years of college. The length of the current marriage ranged from 1 month to 6 years, with an average duration of 22.5 months. Of the subjects, 55 (87.3%) were in their second marriage, only 5 (7.9%) in their first marriage, and 3 (4.8%) in their second remarriage. Of the wives, 28 (87.5%) were stepmothers to their husbands' children, and 22 (71%) of the husbands were stepfathers to their wives' children. The families included 64 children who actually lived in the home, with 35 additional children having some contact with the family but living with another parent. The average number of children per family, including stepchildren, natural children, and children of the current marriage, was 3.3. Eighty-five (81.7%) of the children were under the age of 18.

Subjects were primarily nonclinic families who responded to newspaper articles concerning stepparent issues and the availability of the project. Only three of the couples participating had current involvement with a children's outpatient clinic for difficulties relating to their children.

Measures

The Family Environment Scale (FES) was used to measure perceptions of family climate (Moos, Insel, & Humphrey, 1974). Both Form R (real) and Form I (ideal) were administered. Subjects responded to a short form (first 40 items) of the scale, which yields standard scores on 10 subscales.

The subscales include cohesion, expressiveness, conflict, independence, achievement orientation, intellectual-cultural orientation, active-recreational orientation, moral-religious emphasis, organization, and control. The normative sample for the FES included 185 families primarily from middle and upper-middle socioeconomic levels. Test–retest reliabilities reported by the authors of the scale ranged, for the 10 subscales, from .68 to .86. Additional data concerning reliability and validity of the FES are reported by Moos et al. (1974).

In addition to the FES, a stepparent questionnaire (SQ) developed by the authors was administered. The questionnaire consisted of 12 statements reflecting beliefs about stepparenting that have been reported in the literature. The SQ, designed to assess agreement or disagreement with statements about stepparenting, was used to determine the impact of the information delivered during the session on beliefs about stepparenting held by the participants. The items included statements such as, "If a child has a good relationship with his stepparent, he no longer desires a relationship with his natural parent," and "Stepfamilies are as cohesive and have the same amount of stress as nonstepfamilies."

Procedure

Potential participants contacted the project by telephone and were scheduled for a structured interview during which husbands and wives separately were informed of the purpose and nature of the stepparent sessions. At the time of the structured interview, subjects were assigned to either an experimental group or to a waiting-list control group. The control group subjects were administered measures immediately following the structured interview and again 4 weeks later, after which they began participation in the group sessions. The experimental subjects were administered measures before the first session and immediately following the last session.

THE STEPPARENT GROUP PROCESS

The stepparent group educational sessions consisted of four weekly 1½-hour sessions that included five or six couples. Curriculum for each of the four sessions is described below.

Session 1

The first session began with a restatement of the purpose of the educational group, which was to provide information concerning common issues that stepparents face, as well as a supportive group to share information concerning stepparenting. Each participant was given a packet of reading materials containing articles and references about stepparenting. The format included a lecture followed by a videotape and discussion. During the information section of the first session, parents were informed about good news for stepfamilies. This included, for example, some statements about benefits for children having two sets of parents, as well as the commitment of stepparents to family life and the model of a working marital relationship. Dilemmas for stepparents were also presented, including such problems as attempting to form a relationship with a child too quickly to compensate for the loss of a parent, working out family rules, recognizing unrealistic expectation regarding attachment between children and stepparents, money issues, issues of sexuality in the stepfamily, and dealing with myths, including the wicked stepmother.

The group viewed a short segment of a television program produced by Phil Donahue in which John and Emily Visher, who have published information about stepfamilies (Visher & Visher, 1979) were interviewed together with two stepfamilies. The participants then engaged in a general discussion of the information presented and shared difficulties with each other, as well as successes.

Session 2

The second session used approximately the same format as that of the first session. More specifically, it concentrated on issues concerning children in a stepfamily. Issues included the need to be sensitive to the developmental level of the child and the way in which developmental issues affect stepparenting. For example, the normal disengagement of the child during adolescence and its impact on stepparents were discussed. Other issues reviewed included the problem of children being overly close to one parent as a result of losing the other parent, feelings of loss, divided loyalties, fantasies of reunion of the previous family, and restimulation of anger or guilt. Finally, the parents were shown a 10-minute segment of an interview with a 15-year-old stepchild who discussed her experience during the divorce of her parents and their subsequent remarriages.

The group discussed with each other their reactions to the material presented and shared information concerning difficulties or successes with their children. The group members were asked at the end of the session to determine particular needs and interests for the third session.

Session 3

The third session was designed to provide some flexibility in meeting the specific needs of the group. Members were asked to identify issues of greatest concern to themselves. These issues typically included discipline of children and taking up a role as stepparent. A videotape, approximately 10 minutes long, was shown in response to each group's stated goals for the session. For example, four out of the six groups were shown a couple discussing issues of stepparenting in their families, and the other two groups with wives who had no natural children were presented a videotape in which a stepmother in a similar situation discussed her problems. One group did not want to see a videotape in order to gain more discussion time. During several groups, a research assistant who was a stepchild herself provided information from her experience and answered questions.

Session 4

The fourth session began with a discussion of the importance of the marital relationship and reviewed some difficulties that arise in communication between spouses and relationships with ex-spouses and relatives. Following this brief information section, a graph was given to all participants illustrating their responses on the FES that they had made prior to Session 1. After a brief explanation, the research staff guided each couple individually in looking at and discussing similarities and differences between their perceptions of the family. The group was then asked for feedback regarding the group experience and recommendations for future group experiences for other stepparents. Stepparents were invited to continue contact with the group leaders, and consultation was offered on an ongoing basis when requested.

Follow-up Interviews

All couples were contacted by phone 2–6 months following the sessions and were asked for additional feedback concerning the group experience, as well as current perceptions of family functioning. Ten families were randomly selected for interviews with the children of the family. These children were asked about their current impression of family functioning and any changes noted during the past few months.

RESULTS AND DISCUSSION

FES Dimensions

Differences between current and ideal family perceptions, based on the 10 dimensions yielded by the FES, were evaluated for significance by t tests for paired samples. These tests determined whether or not the 63 subjects reported significantly different current versus ideal perceptions of their families before the group experience and 4 weeks later, after completing either the group or a waiting period. In general, it was found that differences between current and ideal family perceptions were reliably greater than zero and were indeed significant, except for achievement orientation (Table 1). The stepparents in the project, therefore, generally reported (as was hypothesized) that the current social climate of the family was not as they idealized.

These results were consistent with data from structured interviews which suggested that many families who sought involvement in the project were experiencing stress. Of the female participants, 25 (78.1%) and, of the male participants, 22 (71%) reported problems in the family as a result of the remarriage, despite the tendency in stepfamilies to deny major difficulties (Goldstein, 1974). Professionals who seek to establish group experiences for stepparents may wish to make use of objective measures to clarify areas of dissatisfaction. Clinically, it was observed during the final group sessions that feedback concerning discrepancies between what was perceived and idealized led to constructive discussion of problem areas.

Analyses were then performed to determine whether differences between current and ideal family perceptions showed significant changes over time as a function of the group experience. Two-way repeated-measures analyses of variance were employed, with difference scores (ideal minus current perception) for the 10 FES dimensions as dependent variables and group membership (experimental vs. control) and time (first vs. second assessment) as independent variables. Results of the analysis of variance showed no significant Group × Time interaction on any FES

Table 1 *t* Tests for Differences between Current and Ideal Family Perceptions (FES)

Dimension	M Diff	t	p <
Pre			
Cohesion	10.18	5.94	.001
Expressiveness	14.38	6.97	.001
Conflict	−11.92	−6.43	.001
Independence	6.06	3.67	.001
Achievement orientation	−0.71	−0.45	ns
Intellectual-cultural orientation	8.73	6.05	.001
Active-recreational orientation	12.75	8.09	.001
Moral-religious emphasis	5.08	4.86	.001
Organizational orientation	9.32	5.71	.001
Control	−4.02	−2.61	.012
Post			
Cohesion	6.41	3.90	.001
Expressiveness	14.21	6.76	.001
Conflict	−8.03	−4.20	.001
Independence	6.94	3.26	.002
Achievement orientation	1.54	1.32	ns
Intellectual-cultural orientation	7.11	5.36	.001
Active-recreational orientation	14.73	7.94	.001
Moral-religious emphasis	4.48	4.05	.001
Organizational orientation	9.27	5.71	.001
Control	−5.02	−3.45	.002

dimension; that is, changes over time in discrepancy between current and ideal family perceptions occurred independently of whether the subjects had the group experience or were waiting-list controls. Post hoc analyses, however, showed that in the case of discrepancies between current and ideal levels of conflict, subjects who had the group experience changed slightly more over time than control subjects. The results suggest that the group experience affected, in a positive way, the degree of conflict experienced by participating families. There were, finally, significant effects for time alone in current versus ideal perceptions of family cohesion and conflict. Over time, subjects who had the group experience as well as those who were waiting-list controls showed less discrepancy in their perception of current versus ideal family cohesion, $F(1,61) = 4.20$, $p < .05$, and conflict, $F(1,61) = 6.48, p < .01$.

Other analyses of variance were performed to evaluate change, over time, in current perceptions of the family as well as ideal perceptions. First, a significant Group × Time interaction was found for current intellectual–cultural orientation, $F(1,61) = 7.03$, $p < .01$. Subjects who attended the group sessions showed an increase, over time, in their concern about political, social, intellectual, and cultural events, whereas control subjects showed a decrease. Both experimental and control group subjects showed a decrease in their perceived levels of current family conflict, $F(1,61) = 9.65, p < .01$. Time also influenced, in both groups, perceptions of ideal levels of family cohesion, $F(1,61) = 4.19, p < .05$, involvement in active-recreational pursuits, $F(1,61) = 6.08, p < .05$, and control $F(1,61) = 8.10, p < .01$. Subjects in both groups showed a decrease in ideal levels of cohesion and control and an increase in their ideal level of active-recreational involvement.

In summary, group subjects differed little in reported change from control subjects. However, subjects who attended group sessions showed an increase, over time, in intellectual-cultural matters, as well as less discrepancy between current and ideal levels of family conflict. Both groups showed some change over time in certain dimensions of family environment measured by the FES. It appears likely that both groups of subjects, by committing themselves to group educational sessions, had thereby begun a process of change that obscured effects specific to experimental versus control group membership. The effects of the structured interview alone, for example, may have sensitized subjects to stepparent issues.

Stepparent Questionnaire

Stepparent questionnaire responses were also analyzed to determine whether the group experience influenced the extent to which subjects agreed with statements reflecting myths or realities about stepparenting. An analysis of variance failed to yield a significant Group × Time interaction, suggesting no difference in change between experimental and control subjects. However, both groups of subjects showed a highly significant change in attitudes over time, $F(1,61) = 11.06, p < .01$. Other post hoc analyses revealed that this change was more characteristic of experimental subjects to bring their activities concerning stepparenting issues more in line with realities versus myths about stepparenting. The failure to find a significant Group × Time interaction may have related to sensitization of control subjects to stepparenting issues during the 4-week waiting period following the structured interview.

Clinical Evaluation

Based on clinical impressions gathered during the structured interviews and the group sessions, it appeared that many of the couples were experiencing stresses related to their remarriage. Many verbalized problems reflecting a lack of guidelines and preparation for remarriage, a phenomenon previously reported by Messinger (1976). The follow-up conversations with participating families suggested that the greatest perceived benefits of the program were the sharing of mutual problems and the support they received from the group. Both the group experience and the use of videotapes depicting the problems of other members of stepfamilies appeared to decrease anxiety, guilt, and a sense of isolation for group members. As one mother reflected: "I believed the problems we were having were because I was not working hard enough. I can now slow down and take it as it comes."

In addition, the children from 10 families who had been randomly selected and were interviewed had many positive comments about the effects of the group on the family. All but 1 of the 13 children seen said that they felt things were better in their family after their parents attended the four sessions. They made such comments as, "We do more things for fun now," and "My parents are nicer to us now."

Initially, the couples in the group educational sessions expressed a reluctance to resolve issues related to stepparenting. Encouragement to solve problems and the use of feedback via objective measures (the FES) in a supportive atmosphere facilitated an ongoing process of negotiation. In addition, the use of a structured time allotment to confront issues raised in the session paved the way for some participants to raise uncomfortable topics. As one father reported, "We did a lot of talking after the session on the way home about things that had seemed too scary to discuss earlier."

CONCLUSION

In conclusion, the group educational experience was described as beneficial by most of the stepparents. Statistical tests suggested some change as a result of the group in the level of conflict experienced by the families who participated, as well as interest in intellectual-cultural matters. Professionals planning to use the modality are advised that stepparents who seek out the experience may be using the group to facilitate an ongoing process of change. In addition, preexisting differences in current versus ideal family perceptions may be a source of dissatisfaction and should be addressed. Stepparents from lower socioeconomic groups, finally, may not be as likely to seek out such group experience. Further exploration of ways to provide group experiences for these and other groups in the community is encouraged.

REFERENCES

Ahrons, C.R. The continuing coparental relationship between divorced spouses. *American Journal of Orthopsychiatry*, 1981, *51*, 415–428.

Goldstein, H.S. Reconstituted families: The second marriage and its children. *Psychiatric Quarterly*, 1974, *48*, 433–440.

Guerney, L.F., & Wolfgang, G. Long-range evaluation of effects on foster parents of a foster parent skills training program. *Journal of Clinical Psychology*, 1981, *10*, 33–37.

Jacobsen, D.S. Stepfamilies: Myths and realities. *Social Work*, 1979, *24*, 202–207.

Kagey, J.R., Vivace, S., & Lutz, W. Mental health primary prevention: The role of parent mutual support groups, 1981, *71*, 166–167.

Messinger, L. Remarriage between divorced people with children from previous marriages: A proposal for preparation for remarriage. *Journal of Marriage and Family Counseling*, 1976, *2*, 193–200.

Messinger, L., & Walker, K.N. From marriage breakdown to remarriage: Parental tasks and therapeutic guidelines. *American Journal of Orthopsychiatry*, 1981, *51*, 429–438.

Moos, R.H., Insel, P.M., & Humphrey, B. *Preliminary Manual for Family Environment Scale, Work Environment Scale, Group Environment Scale*. Palo Alto, Calif.: Consulting Psychologists Press, 1974.

Mowatt, M.H. Group psychotherapy for stepfathers and their wives. *Psychotherapy: Theory, Research, and Practice*, 1972, *9*, 328–331.

Ransom, J.W., Schlesinger, S., & Derdeyn, A.P. A stepfamily in formation. *American Journal of Orthopsychiatry*, 1979, *49*, 36–43.

Sager, C.J., Walker, E., Brown, H.S., Crohn, H.M., & Rodstein, E. Improving functioning of the remarried family system. *Journal of Marital and Family Therapy*, 1981, *7*, 3–13.

Visher, E.B., & Visher, J.S. Major areas of difficulty for stepparent couples. *International Journal of Family Counseling*, 1978, *6*, 70–80.

Visher, E.B., & Visher, J.S. *Stepfamilies: A guide to working with stepparents and stepchildren*. New York: Brunner/Mazel, 1979.

Walker, K.N., & Messinger, L. Remarriage after divorce: Dissolution and reconstruction of family boundaries. *Family Process*, 1979, *18*, 185–192.

11. A Basis for Understanding and Treating the Remarried Family

Helen Crohn, M.S.S.
Jewish Board of Family and Children's Services
New York, New York

Clifford J. Sager, M.D.
Family Psychiatry and the Remarried Consultation Service
Jewish Board of Family and Children's Services
New York, New York

Holly Brown, R.N.
Advanced Family Therapy Training Program
Jewish Board of Family and Children's Services
New York, New York

Evelyn Rodstein, M.S.W.
Jewish Board of Family and Children's Services
New York, New York

Libby Walker, M.S.W.
Private Practice
New York, New York

Eleven

BECAUSE OF AN INCREASING AWARENESS THAT THE NEEDS OF the remarried families (also known as Rem,* blended, second, reconstituted, or stepfamilies) seen in our clinic were not the same as the needs of the intact family, a special service, the Remarried Consultation Service, with its own interdisciplinary team was established in 1976.[1] Through clinical and personal experience, we sought to define and then disseminate to others the ways in which the Rem family differed from the nuclear family in structure and dynamics and to develop improved therapeutic and preventative methods. A preliminary[2] research project was done with the service's case families. A review was conducted for ourselves and others of knowledge about Rem, its treatment, and the prophylaxis of dysfunction.[3] The team provided much needed peer supervision, sharing of ideas, and personal support in working with Rem families in which multiple crises, confusion, and complexity often occur.[4]

DEFINITION OF REM FAMILY SUPRASYSTEM AND SUBSYSTEMS

A Rem family is created by the marriage or the living together in a committed relationship (LTCR) of two persons, one or both of whom were previously married or LTCR and are now separated, divorced, or widowed, and who may or may not have children of the previous union living in or visiting. The couple and the children, mutual, custodial, and

---

*Pertaining to a remarriage situation.

visiting, form the Rem family subsystem, which has intrahousehold components, the remarried couple and the mutual child, and interhousehold components, visiting in or out, custodial and noncustodial children. As a household, the Rem family subsystem changes in a patterned way as children come and go. At the same time in which the Rem family subsystem is evolving through its life cycle, the Rem couple is evolving through its marital life cycle and the individuals in the family are progressing in their personal life cycles.

The Rem family suprasystem is composed of the Rem family subsystem plus former spouses, grandparents, stepgrandparents, aunts, uncles, and others who may have significant input into the Rem family subsystem. Provided both biological parents are living, the children who ferry back and forth are part of each of their biological parents' households. Because of the high rate of divorce and remarriage, both the Rem family subsystem and the Rem family suprasystem have become common family forms.

The Positive Potential of Rem Experience

A successful Rem family has a great deal to offer adults and children. It provides exposure to a variety of life styles, opinions, feelings, and enriching relationships. In Rem, an adult forms a new love relationship with a partner, which is often strengthened by maturity, life experience, and stability in identity and grows through the gaining of independence and free choice as opposed to desperation and fear. The previously divorced adult, wiser from hindsight, forms a new type of marital relationship, with the opportunity to parent and to benefit from a supportive suprasystem. In Rem, children can learn to appreciate and respect differences in people and ways of living, can receive affection and support from a new stepparent and the new suprasystem, and can observe the remarried parent in a good and loving marital relationship, using this as a model for their own future love relationships. If an only child, he or she may gain the experience of cooperation that a subsystem with other children offers.

Structural Differences between Rem and Nuclear Families

People in Rem families and Rem therapists are continuously reminded of, if not surprised by, the differences between the nuclear and Rem family. Denial of or confusion about these differences can cause additional stress for the family and therapist alike.

Marital and Parenting Tasks

In a nuclear family there are two adults and one or more children who are progeny of the adults; the marital pair predates the parental pair; and the marital and parental tasks are shared by the same two adults. A Rem family subsystem consists of two adults and one or more children, but each child has been parented by only one of the adults; the parent–child unit predates the Rem marital pair; and the marital and parental tasks are not shared by the same two adults—parenting tasks are shared with each divorced adult's previous spouse or spouses. Hence, at least three adults are involved with parenting each child, often four adults when each natural parent has remarried, and possibly as many as six adults in the event of third marriages.

Case 1 (Multiple parents)
Adam Wise, now 15, resides with his father, Jack Wise, and his woman friend, whom Mr. Wise is planning to marry shortly. This will be Mr. Wise's fourth marriage. He has a son, now 20, from the first marriage, whom Adam sees occasionally. Adam is the product of Mr. Wise's second marriage, which lasted until Adam was 3. He lived with his mother and visited his father until age 6; then, at the advice of the mother's therapist, the father took custody of Adam, who then visited his mother. Shortly thereafter, Mr. Wise married Miss Hughes, with whom he had been living for several years. She took a strong parenting role with Adam, structuring his life as well as that of her husband. Mr. Wise and his third wife separated when Adam was 13; in those 7 years Adam had become very attached to her while continuing to see his mother weekly. Mr. Wise and Adam's mother were still locked in a hostile battle, so Mr. Wise's third wife had gradually related to Adam's mother around issues of Adam, instead of her husband's doing so.

In their separation agreement, Mr. Wise and his third wife recognized Adam's special attachment and need for his stepmother, so that regular visiting was arranged. The stepmother pushed for this, since she was "ending a bad marriage but not wanting to give Adam up too."

At present, Adam lives with his father and his father's fourth wife (second stepmother) during the week. He has dinner with his stepmother once a week and spends Sunday with her if he wishes. He visits his mother every Saturday. He will spend a week's vacation this year each with mother and stepmother.

None of the women in this suprasystem have remarried or had more children. Adam at present relates to four adults as parents: his father, his mother, his first stepmother, and his second stepmother.

Membership, Boundaries, Roles, and Rules

In a nuclear family, members belong in only one family system, which is relatively closed regarding inclusion of members. Internal is clearly delineated from external. There is input from significant others, but this is usually experienced positively as family. If both adult partners have sufficiently individuated from their families of origin, the input from significant others is less likely to contribute to system malfunction. Family expectations, rules, roles, tasks, and purposes are also clear. They conform with the generational boundaries and sexual taboos defined by society.

In contrast, membership in the Rem family subsystem is open to interpretation. Some members may belong in two systems or they may feel they do not belong at all in the unit. The subsystem has permeable boundaries (Messinger, 1976) and significant input from others in the suprasystem. Not only former spouses, grandparents, and children, but institutions can have a marked impact on the Rem family's viability and functioning. Generational and sexual boundaries are often vague and can more easily be trespassed. Expectations, rules, roles, and tasks in the Rem system have remained ill-defined by society. Each Rem system has had to generate itself without a model.

Case 2 (Permeable Boundaries, Role Confusion)
Mr. Horn, age 40, was divorced from his first wife and had three boys, ages 15, 13, and 8, in his custody since their mother had chronic schizophrenia with repeated hospitalizations. He then married Miss Page, who was then 26 years old with no previous marriage or children. Mrs. Page-Horn took charge of raising the three boys who had been living like waifs with their father. Mr. Horn's ex-wife visited with the boys in their home as she had no established residence. This became a source of intrusion, and Mrs. Page-Horn wanted these visits terminated. Her parents, the children's step-grandparents, agreed (they also had been giving financial help). The Horns gradually were able to set more limits on the mother's intrusions.

Five years later, the oldest boy married and moved out; the middle boy now 18, blossomed into a handsome athletic boy. When the youngest boy reached 13, Mrs. Page-Horn retreated from the mothering role, wanting to pursue her own career as an artist. The parenting role was not picked up by her husband, who was also absorbed in his artistic career. He had aged considerably, and Mrs. Page-Horn found herself attracted to younger men, including her stepson who was flirtatious with her. The youngest boy, now parentless, began to be truant from school and was depressed.

This complicated Rem family illustrates some of the complexities due to intrusion, ill-defined roles, and poor generational and sexual boundaries.

Purposes of the Family System

In a nuclear family, the couple seeks to establish a marital partnership in which needs for companionship, sexual and emotional intimacy, financial and emotional support, and individuation are met. In addition, the nuclear family usually has procreation of offspring and the establishment of a nurturing environment for children as purposes. Both partners of the couple usually start out at similar individual life cycle stages, allowing dovetailing of marital life cycle and family life cycle tasks.[5]

In the Rem family subsystem, the couple also seeks to establish a marital partnership in which fulfillment of needs for companionship, emotional and sexual intimacy, financial support, and individuation are possible. But unlike the nuclear family, the Rem family has an underpinning of experience of failure (divorce) or loss (death of former spouse). Such experience can have a powerful effect on the ability to meet needs in the Rem coupling. Procreation is not always a purpose in Rem because the family already exists; the consolidation of the Rem couple also becomes harder to achieve because of the influence of the suprasystem, particularly ex-spouses.

In Rem, the couple often is not congruent in their individual life cycle phases, and there is concomitant disruption in the marital life cycle. Sharp differences in significant areas, for example, the wish to have a mutual child, may emerge. We think of the member or members of the Rem couple who were married before as adding a new marital life cycle track while the original marital life cycle with their former spouse or spouses continues, for example, around parenting tasks. In addition, in Rem, individual and family life cycle tasks may clash; for example, as the Rem unit seeks to consolidate itself, adolescent members may be seeking greater autonomy, personal space, and primary relationship to peers, not family members.

Case 3 (Purpose/life cycle conflicts in Rem)

Mr. Cross is a boyish-looking 45-year-old executive in the investment business who had lived with his sons, now 23 and 21, until his divorce 9 years ago. At the time of requesting help, he and the second Mrs. Cross, a 32-year-old fashion editor, who had not been previously married, had just celebrated their sixth wedding anniversary. Both members of the couple were hard-driving professionals, and this maintained a balance in the relationship. The couple's anniversary coincided with Mrs. Cross' physician's suggestion that she try to conceive, with Mr. Cross achieving a promotion, Mrs. Cross' younger sister having a baby, and Mr. Cross' older son's announcing his engagement.

The couple had discussed having a child prior to their marriage. Mr. Cross said he would consider it. At this point, Mrs. Cross was adamant that the time was ripe. Mr. Cross had done some soul searching of the pleasures and pains of raising his sons and was sure that he did not want another child at his stage of life. Mrs. Cross remained firm in her decision, and when attempts to convince each other failed, the couple opted for divorce while exploring the dilemma of dissolving a basically good marriage. Explaining the dilemma in the context of needs no longer being met enough to continue and a life cycle conflict that was unresolvable helped the couple put their situation in perspective.

ENTRY TO TREATMENT

Treatment with the clinical population of Rem families can be an effective and exciting process for family and therapist but can be also a time-consuming one because of the complexity of the family systems involved. Instead of having been a system that functioned well at one time and then began to malfunction, Rem families often have not been able to consolidate themselves into a viable functioning unit except perhaps for a brief honeymoon period. Characteristically, these families call for help when in crisis and desperate. It is not uncommon for a family to arrive at the point of having expelled a member, often an adolescent, or when the couple is verging on separation. The pressure on the therapist to try to immediately rectify the situation is tremendous and must be resisted. The following discussion focuses on situations in which a child or children are the identified problem, and consequently where there would be an indication to involve the suprasystem as soon as possible.[6]

Initial Phase: Telephone Calls—Whom to Include

Most often the custodial parent, or if the custodial parent has remarried, the stepparent, will call about difficulties with a child or an adolescent. The second most frequent initiator is the visited parent.

Therapy starts with the first phone call. We attend to the present emergency, simultaneously beginning the process of evaluating the family system. Regardless of what else may be transacted in the first contact, the mere seeking and ordering of information, when it is a shared process, brings knowledge, intelligence, and structure to the family members as it does to the therapist.

As with nuclear families, in the initial phase the therapist has the greatest leverage to involve everyone who is part of or who affects the family system. Once therapy has begun, it is often more difficult to include a former spouse because the therapist is likely to be viewed with hostility and identified as being on the side of the Rem system. We see all members who ask for help if we cannot enlist the others at the start. In the process that ensues, the Rem family suprasystem learns how interrelated it is and when and how to disengage appropriately.

Whoever calls for help about a child, whether it be the parent or stepparent, we make every effort to include both parents and stepparents from the outset. Frequently, clients will articulate anxiety about including their former mate, or the stepparent might be anxious or jealous about being present with the former spouse due to ex-spouse hostilities or hidden collusive affection. The therapist should note the concern and point out that since the child lives with both families, it is in the best interests of the child for the adults to work together, and that it is the parenting and stepparenting issues, not the ex-marital hurts or financial issues, that will be addressed. The therapist is active in setting clear limits in sessions that include ex-spouses and stepparents. Only when all adults agree should one include in the therapeutic contract attempts to resolve residual pain and anger from the former marriage or to put residual affection and love into appropriate perspective.

Work with the suprasystem requires therapeutic flexibility. It may be necessary to see each biological parent separately to establish a connection and promote comfort with the therapist before setting up joint meetings. If the therapist is already identified with one partner of the system, it may be necessary initially to enlist a cotherapist to make the connection to the other partner, who may have been excluded. Sometimes we employ an adaptation of MacGregor and his colleagues' (1964) multiple-impact family therapy by assigning a different therapist to each subsystem of the suprasystem. However, this is a costly luxury that cannot be continued for a long period of time.

Setting up the initial session takes effort on the part of the therapist and an ability to be able to make connections on the telephone with various parts of the suprasystem. The telephone work takes skill, perspective, and knowledge of Rem systems—it is not an impersonal process, but a chance to make an initial connection.

Use of the Genogram: The First Sessions

The genogram is a family map that we employ to quickly understand the complicated structure of the Rem family we are about to see.[7] Sometimes, we sketch a rough genogram during the initial telephone call to be able to speak knowledgeably and clearly about the family. A more complete genogram is then drawn with the Rem family sometime during the initial session.

We find that the multiple changes that have occurred, and most likely the multiple losses also, as dramatically highlighted by the genogram, may facilitate a delayed mourning reaction in some family members. We inquire about the children's biological parents, even if one of them is not present, to soften any loyalty conflict a child may have between the parents and stepparents and to support the child's needed connection to both. The therapist's implicit and explicit recognition of the other important persons in the child's life does more than any statement could. Information specific to the Rem situation can be asked for directly or deduced from observation and interaction, including data on—

- The present Rem unit: living-in, living-out, and visiting children, when they visit, how often, holiday schedules, who makes school visits on parent's day, and other sensitive living arrangements in the household

- How the present Rem unit was formed: the background of the couple's meeting and courtship; how and if the children were prepared for the remarriage; if the former partner or partners knew of the remarriage and by whom they were informed; changes in residence, financial arrangements, and other parameters
- The two single-parent household structures: the quality and quantity of time spent with each child by each parent, the role of grandparents, and the relation between the separated spouses during this period
- The original nuclear family system: when, why, and how this was dissolved, what each adult and child's understanding of that dissolution was in the past and currently, and dates of actual physical separation and of the legal divorce
- The families of origin of all adults, both Rem spouses and former spouses, and assessment of input by each significant person, both current and past.

It is important to observe overt and covert alliances, power structures, levels of intimacy and bonds between members, and patterns of inclusion and exclusion in the system. However, one need not be compulsive about history taking: basic facts first, then the rest unfolds as therapy goes on. Two other areas in Rem are crucial to learn about as rapidly as possible: mate choice and life cycles. This is usually revealed in individual and couple sessions with adults and by use of the marital contract with the Rem couple.

1. Mate Choice: the factors, unconscious as well as conscious, determining mate choice for the second as well as the first marriage. Did those married more than once learn from past experiences; does the remarriage reflect a positive change in their level of maturity; are there reasonable expectations and goals? Are the two individual marriage contracts of the couple concordant, complementary, or in conflict? (Sager, 1976).

2. Life Cycles—individual, marital, and family: Are the life cycle needs of each marital partner consistent with the other partner's and with the needs of the Rem family? At what stage are the individuals in the life cycle of their former families and their former marriages? In addition, when a child is the presenting problem, we examine the difficulty on the family systems level, as well as whether the difficulty predated Rem. What part did constitutional and developmental

factors play in the child's problem? What is reactive to separation, divorce, and remarriage? What is developing from malfunction in the parental system and in the suprasystem, and what parts of the problem are independent of these?

Treatment Goals

Treatment goals are not simple, they reflect the multiple levels of determinants of behavior: expressed, unexpressed, preconscious, and unconscious. The therapist must be alert to the desires beyond awareness that put obstacles in the way of attaining expressed goals. Masochistic or self-defeating needs can be revealed during anamnestic data collection by noting self-defeating patterns in behavior and interactions observed in the family sessions. Often such patterns can be bypassed in therapy. As change begins to occur, the therapist should expect to see resistance initiated by the obstructor, often with the unconscious collusion of other system members. If negative goals cannot be bypassed, they must be brought into the open and dealt with more directly. This is one of the many complexities of human system behavior that defeats attempts at cookbook therapy and requires a broad spectrum of skills and knowledge.

There are immediate, intermediate, and long-range treatment goals. Individuals and the family as a system are helped to define achievable goals. For example, when a child says, "I want to feel like I felt when my parents were married," it usually means "I want my parents reunited," a goal that cannot be attained. One then tries to help the child to achieve a more reasonable goal: accepting the loss and irretrievability of the original nuclear family, experiencing the anger and sadness that leads to acceptance, and experiencing both the positive and negative aspects of the present Rem family.

The therapist, too, may have goals that must be shared with the family. Those goals that are decided on must be agreed to by all involved. Goals and contracts are under constant evaluation and review as treatment progresses; this work forms the essence of the therapeutic process.

Common treatment goals with Rem families include many that are premised on acceptance and enhancement of the effectiveness of the suprasystem. For example, an early goal may be to end the scapegoating of a child. This might be approached by helping former spouses and their families to eschew fixing blame for the termination of the former marriage. Then adult anger can be worked through or more readily bypassed for the children's needs. Guilt or retribution for past acts need not be used as motivation for current action, thus allowing parents and stepparents to share some responsibility for child rearing. Some other goals frequently encountered are the following:

- to consolidate the Rem couple as a unit and establish their authority in the system
- to consolidate the parental authority in the system among natural parents and stepparents with the formation of a collaborative coparenting team
- as a corollary to item 2, to help children deal with and minimize the continuance and exacerbation of loyalty binds
- to facilitate mourning of the nuclear family, former partner, old neighborhoods, friends, and way of life
- to be certain that there is a secure place for the child's development through optimal use of the entire suprasystem; to help meet the individual life cycle needs of the child, even when these conflict with family and marital life cycle needs,
- to help family members accept and tolerate the differences between Rem and an idealized intact family model.

The latter include differences in control of money, control of children, feelings for and of the natural parent and stepparent, rules and expectations in two households, and levels of bonding. Therapy is structured to achieve goals in as orderly a progression as possible, accented by a dash of the serendipitous. Rarely have we had a treatment plan, however, that did not have to be revised (Sager, 1957). Goals of the two parental systems may be mutually exclusive, as may be those of any subsystem or individual vis-à-vis another. These goal differences must be clearly delineated to determine if they are real or apparent. If real, can they be reconciled or negotiated in some fashion? Some are so pervasive and mutually exclusive that family members and the therapist may have to accept that the system is not viable, as illustrated in Case 3 above, where irreconcilable life cycle differences necessitated marital dissolution.

TREATMENT

There are three general theoretical systems of psychological treatment that are available: (a) insight methods, (b) methods based on general systems theory, and (c) approaches derived from learning theory, such as behavior modification methods. Although many of our techniques are based on family and suprafamily systems, knowledge of individual intrapsychic dynamics, human development, and couple dynamics is also used to determine some of the interventions, as well as using tasks and positive reinforcement techniques. The individual should not become lost in the system; neither should the therapist lose sight of the power of the family system to shape and alter behavior.

Common Treatment Issues in Rem Therapy: Adult Pairing and Parent–Child Love

We have referred previously to some Rem couples' inability to consolidate into a viable marital unit, meeting both the love needs of the adults while meeting the love needs of the children and carrying on with parenting and other appropriate family needs. Often there are bonds and priorities as powerful or more powerful elsewhere that can produce crisis, confusion, and jealousy in the current Rem couple relationship. Such factors may lead to a concomitant failure to resolve pivotal marital issues of intimacy, power, exclusion–inclusion of others, and failure to negotiate and resolve individual and joint marital contracts (Sager, 1976; Sager & Hunt, 1979).

These failures may have come about through a variety of circumstances. Parents often experience guilt or confusion between loyalty to their children of a former spouse and to their current spouse. The parent, not the child or new spouse, must take prime responsibility for confronting and resolving this dilemma. One partner may have failed to mourn, appropriately work through, and accept the loss of his or her former spouse. Other couples may be involved in a bond of either pseudomutuality or pseudohostility (Wynne et al., 1958). This bond inevitably intrudes into the relationship. Conversely, the former spouse may have refused to accept termination of the marital relationship, and may constantly intrude into the current pairing, using the children for this purpose. The remarried partner may covertly condone this intrusion out of guilt over the end of the previous marriage. When a former spouse intrudes, the marital bond of the present couple is defused.

Some parents develop an overly close bond to a child during the initial household phase in which both parents are single. Later, neither the parent nor the child is able to alter the quality and intensity of this bond to make room for the entry and inclusion of the new marital partner into the system. It is a process that usually takes time and patience. The new marital partners may be unable or unwilling to help their mates separate from the child and move into a closer couple pairing without arousing defensiveness and drawing hostility onto themselves. The difficulty in keeping the adult-pairing love separate from parent–child love reappears as a common problem of Rem families.

Issues for Children

To the child remarriage represents finality and the loss of a dream of reinstating the old family. The wedding is not a joyous event; it is a time of renewed loss, sometimes experienced by the child as a second parental divorce. Acceptance of the reality of Rem may be postponed if the child enters into disruptive denial or undoing maneuvers. When the exclusive relationship with the parent ends, the child must move over to make room for others. At the same time, loyalty bonds may range from mild to extreme. Good feelings a child experiences toward a stepparent may have to be repressed because they represent disloyalty to the same-sex parent. Positive expectations that the child has for the Rem family and new stepparent, both expressed and unexpressed, may cause conflict with the expectations of others; most commonly, a child may expect the stepparent to be a friend or have a peerlike relationship, but the stepparent may precipitously become authoritarian.

When a child gains stepsiblings, differences in background, culture, life experience, privilege, intellect, and artistic and physical abilities emerge, and the children feel the pressure of these differences. The child may have changed ordinal position, from the youngest to one of the older children, and resultant expectations can change, causing additional stress on an already stressed child.

Case 4 Unconsolidated Rem Couple; Unresolved Mourning in Child
　　　　and Adult
　　The Starr family applied for therapy for Mrs. Starr's 15-year-old son Tony, who had been depressed for several months, staying home from school and doing poorly in socializing. Mr. and Mrs. Starr had been married for 3 months; Mrs. Starr's first husband died 3 years earlier of cancer. Tony had been adopted as an infant. Mr. Starr was divorced 1 year ago from his first wife, with whom he had a 16-year-old boy, Jeff, who lived with him, and an 18-year-old girl, who lived

with his former wife. Significant in the immediate situation was that Tony and his mother had left their old neighborhood to live in Mr. Starr's family home. Tony had been very involved with his peer group in his former neighborhood, but made only barely passing grades since entering junior high school. The Rem family was fragmented, with the two adolescent stepsiblings avoiding each other in the household; Jeff felt that Mrs. Starr and Tony intruded on his home. Tony had no moorings—he had not attached himself at all and longed to return to his old neighborhood where his paternal grandmother still lived. The remarriage brought to a head for him the unresolved mourning for his deceased father and then on a deeper level for his real mother, whom he fantasized was a movie star who could not keep him. Thus, Tony met his new family not with hostility but a bland indifference and withdrawal from contact.

The couple was unconsolidated. Symbolically, represented by Mr. Starr's procrastination on refurnishing the home as he had promised, they continued to live with the trappings of his former marriage. Mrs. Starr was extremely supportive of him in his frequent depressive states, which were related to his not being able to accept his wife's leaving him and the breakup of the ideal family he thought they had.

Mr. Starr's unresolved mourning was expressed in his not being able to reach out to Tony and in unconsciously giving Jeff the message to stay away. Treatment of the couple involved helping Mr. Starr begin the process of emotional divorce and Mrs. Starr assert her needs with him more forcefully. As they were able to do this, the two stepsiblings began to relate as the stepfather and Tony did.

Treatment Modalities

Starting with knowledge of family systems theory and a conviction regarding the correctness of the concept of multiple genetic and environmental inputs to all individuals and family systems, we work with the Rem family, keeping in mind family structure and individual function, values, and adaptations. Some issues are specific to Rem families; emotional and interactional family system dynamics are more generalized. The idea, both for evaluation and treatment, is to conceptualize the problems in terms of the Rem family suprasystem, keeping in mind the needs of the individual members and the two biological parent systems as well as the specific Rem unit. The primary therapeutic process is to refocus and redefine the problem with the family in terms of the whole suprasystem, its subsequent needs, and its responsibilities. The therapist helps the family understand the expanded system: its differences from a nuclear family and the appropriate significance and role, if any, of the suprasystem's nonhousehold members. Helping the family understand the system facilitates de-scapegoating children, who may be blamed for the Rem family's troubles. Insight methods are used if and when the therapist views them as applicable. When therapeutic tasks are assigned one should be concerned with any resistance to carry them out, the feelings evoked by them, and the actual effects on individuals and the system of having completed them. The reasons for and feelings surfaced by an incompleted task are often of great therapeutic import. The therapist should choose tasks that are designed to produce a specifically predicted behavioral or attitudinal change.

Key treatment questions include whom to include, when, for what purposes, and which treatment modalities to use, when, and for what ends. There are no hard-and-fast rules, and timing is of the essence. Familiarity and ease in working with a variety of modalities are helpful. Beginning immediately with everyone involved in the problem and then working down, breaking into subunits, is easier than beginning with the microsystem (e.g., the child), and trying to include others later. If the Rem couple relationship is the presenting problem and the children are not involved, but there is clearly unfinished business with a prior partner, then a few sessions with the divorced pair or individual sessions with the Rem partner may be necessary to help work out the divorce while moving into couples' work with the current partners. All suprasystem or Rem suprasystem members are not necessarily included in every session. However, the different subsystems and how the present parts fit into the dynamic mosaic are kept in mind.

The capacity for both flexibility and activity on the part of the therapist is crucial; successful treatment depends on the therapist's comfort with moving in and out of the different parts of the system easily and with treatment in different modalities, including family, couple, individual, and child, as indicated. Because emotions in Rem families often run high, the therapist must be comfortable with being active and able to take charge of the sessions. These abilities are particularly necessary when (a) the session includes the former spouse, (b) there is a psychotic individual,

(c) members are manipulative or form an alliance to defeat the therapist, or (d) the family's underlying feelings of hopelessness and despair are rampant.

Multiple Impact Therapy with Families

At times a modified multiple-impact therapy model (MacGregor et al., 1964) is used with Rem suprasystems. A different therapist is assigned to work with, support, and model for separate subsystems, such as children, a former ex-spouse, or grandparents. In a large conjoint meeting the therapist may then act as supporter, interpreter, advocate, negotiator, and spokesperson, as well as therapist, for that part of the system. This modality is particularly helpful with extremely chaotic, polarized, or conflicted systems, or when individuals are unable to enter treatment, which they may consider hostile territory, without the added support of their therapist. It is also recommended for large systems; for instance, when both natural parents are remarried and have several children with needs different from those of the original and the new family. It may be necessary to use this modality only initially around a crisis, and for a brief period until some resolution takes place and clear goals are agreed upon. Ongoing treatment may then proceed as usual.

We try not to use cotherapists unless absolutely necessary (e.g., when there is strong conflict between one subunit and another). Cotherapy is often prohibitively expensive. A solo therapist can achieve similar results through separate appointments with different subsystems of the suprasystem (e.g., with the Rem family subsystem and with the single-parent subsystem). Another excellent way is to split a session, seeing one subsystem for part of the session, the second subsystem for another part of the session, and then both together.

The Use of Groups

Couples' groups are often the treatment of choice for many Rem couples. This modality best addresses several important problem sources in the Rem system, notably, the lack of consolidation of the couple, ill-defined mourning of the lost relationship and spouse, and guilt and conflict about children. The group can provide a structure for the couples apart from their children and stepchildren. It provides time and privacy to work on mutual contracts and support from others in the same situation, struggling with similar issues. At the same time the children have the opportunity to be reparented in a corrective emotional experience with the therapist and one another. With rigid couples who become stuck in conjoint couple sessions, we recommend this change in modality. Family meetings separate from the group can be held periodically, both for the purpose of helping the couple integrate their changes into the system and to facilitate the children's integration into the Rem family.

We have tried multiple-family therapy (MFT) groups (Lacquer, 1972) of unselected Rem families but do not recommend this modality for families who are chaotic and emotionally needy. Further, MFT makes it more difficult to include former spouses and other family suprasystem members because to include them makes the group unwieldy and is disruptive of ongoing processes, as many suprasystem members need to be only transiently engaged in treatment. Adolescents, though, have found MFT to be beneficial. As a result we currently advocate couples' groups and separate groups for children of Rem, particularly for adolescents, who often feel like orphans in their Rem families and are also isolated from their peer group.

We are also experimenting with including the children in the couples' groups for some sessions after the couples have been successful at consolidating themselves and are then ready to address the parenting issues directly, within the supportive framework of the group.

THE THERAPIST

Therapists working with Rem family systems are subjected to constant confrontation with their own emotions and value systems. The first area of emotional assault on the therapist has to do with male–female relatedness and systems of loyalties and consanguinity. The therapist may have values markedly different from those that have allowed Rem adults to divorce and remarry, live with someone, or terminate a marriage. Actions and feelings of various Rem family members touch off emotional reactions based on experiences that the therapist has had, has feared will happen, or has not dared to bring about in his or her own life because of guilt, anxiety, superego constraints, or cultural considerations. True countertransferential reactions may also occur when patients or their systems enmesh the therapist, who reacts the way an individual or system unconsciously set him or her up to react.

The most common areas of vulnerability for therapists are (a) unrealistic expectations—the therapist buys into the fantasies that this Rem family will be perfect; (b) denial—the therapist joins the family in pseudomutuality and denial of differences; (c) abandonment fears—the therapist's own abandonment anxieties are triggered by the issue of loss; (d) control issues—the therapist attempts to allay his or her anxiety by being over-controlling.

The complexities of Rem systems, the sense of despair, hopelessness, and loss, and the chaos and crisis that are at work may spill over into the therapist's personal life. They find themselves putting their personal relationships on hold and avoiding decisions about making or ending commitments to others. In our team depression and despair were common reac· tions without clarity about the source of these feelings, as were making moralistic judgments about clients.

Such reactions can best be dealt with through the use of a trusting and supportive group of peers, which is provided for the staff. Consultation, supervision, and the use of the peer group to help individual therapists to resolve personal reactions have mitigated some of the anxiety and pain that seem to be built into the work with Rem systems.

At the same time the team approach has facilitated consolidation of clinic families, who feel cared about, special to the unit, and less isolated once they know a specialized team of therapists is supporting them.

THERAPIST'S NOTEBOOK—A REM CASE PROCESS

The initial contact was from Linda's aunt, Mrs. Connolly. Linda was 11½. The chief complaint from the aunt was that Linda's mother, Mrs. Alden, divorced for the second time, had been living with her boyfriend, Mr. Samuels, for 1 year. "No one is sure what is really happening to Linda," stated the aunt. Mrs. Alden is 30; Linda had lived with her aunt, Mrs. Connolly, with her maternal grandparents, and with two unmarried uncles. Linda's father is unknown to her; her stepfather and mother separated 1 year ago, after a marriage of 5 years. (See Figure 1.)

Mrs. Connolly was advised to have Linda's mother call the therapist directly. However, the next telephone call came from the maternal grandmother, Mrs. Grace, who stated that Linda's mother will not call or come in. The aunt and the grandmother were advised that we would not be able to see Linda without her mother. Since all of the people we mentioned had been involved in parenting Linda, the therapist suggested that it would be most helpful to have everyone in an initial session (i.e., to include Linda, her mother, mother's boyfriend, the aunt, the two uncles, maternal grandmother, and grandfather). The callers were encouraged to "try again with Mrs. Alden," and were coached on the telephone about ways to approach her. Mrs. Alden finally called and was very angry that her mother and sister had telephoned the Agency. She felt that they were meddling. Yet with a chance to ventilate and gain empathy she begrudgingly agreed to come for a session with everyone present. Prior to the initial session, there was another telephone call from the grandmother, saying that the grandfather did not want to come; his presence was urged and she recounted with "He's always late anyway." The therapist told her that it was extremely important that he attend, and that much could not be done without him. (It had been learned during previous calls that the grandfather had been the head of the household when Linda lived there and that he had given money to Mrs. Alden and Mr. Samuels to buy their present apartment.) The grandmother agreed to urge grandfather to attend.

The aunt then called to say that her husband, a pediatrician, would be unable to attend the session due to work commitment. His attendance was not stressed, since he was considered peripheral. The aunt had one child who the therapist had also decided not to include. Due to the complexity of the system, a second therapist who had received some of the phone calls was employed.

This was an Irish-American, Catholic, middle-class family.

First Session

In the waiting room, the grandfather was absent. The therapists were told by the family that "grandfather is always late." Mrs. Alden and Mr. Samuels were sitting together; on the other side of the room were the grandmother, Mrs. Connolly, Uncle Charles (unmarried, age 27), and Linda. The other uncle had left town on business. The family wanted to start the session, but the cotherapists decided to wait; the grandfather arrived about 20 minutes late.

It was striking that Linda appeared at least 4 years older than her stated age in physical development, poise, and assertiveness. During the initial phase of the session, she aggressively voiced her dislike of Mr. Samuels and how he was ruining her and her mother's life. Linda seemed to have an overly central position in the whole system. Mr. Samuels was a rather tense man who was hostile to Linda; Linda's mother was an attractive but

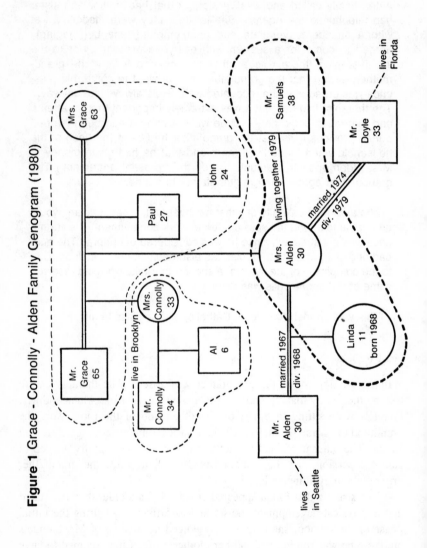

Figure 1 Grace - Connolly - Alden Family Genogram (1980)

somewhat childlike woman. Linda had a tough outer core and a street attitude that proved later to be masking the pain of previous abandonment by her father, her first stepfather, and her mother's inadequate parenting. Linda persisted in her request for her mother to be a stronger figure and stand up to Mr. Samuels. The grandmother was a talkative, involved woman; grandfather was the patriarchal leader of the clan. Mrs. Connolly appeared depressed; Uncle Charles quiet.

This was a highly enmeshed extended family. It was clear that the involvement in their business venture and each other by Mrs. Alden and Mr. Samuels allowed little time for the nurturing and structuring that this bright, energetic, 11 year old needed. It was also clear that Linda was counterphobic regarding her dependency needs, hence the pseudomature stance. The grandparents and aunt were concerned but in an overly intrusive, disruptive way. Each was competing for Linda's affection, putting her mother down in the process. The uncles were peripheral to the action.

It was decided, because of the grandfather's primacy, to invite the male head of the Remarriage Consultation Service to the next session as an authority figure who could meet grandfather on equal terms. The impression was that without the grandfather's approval to proceed, therapy would be undermined. Some initial impressions were given the family with the suggestion that another family suprasystem session be held with the director of the service.

Second Session

All attended on time. The male therapist was supportive of the grandfather's important role with the three generations. During this session, it became clearer that Linda felt that she had the power to determine her mother's romantic involvements. This cued the therapists to possible conflict between the couple. It was suggested to have several couple sessions to explore their commitment. Linda resisted this and was resentful of being excluded. She was offered and refused an exploratory session alone. The grandfather said he would not be able to attend subsequent sessions because of his work schedule. The therapists felt that he was not likely to sabotage treatment; it was decided to work with Linda, Mrs. Alden, and Mr. Samuels after several couple sessions.

Couple Sessions

The couple sessions uncovered an extremely unstable relationship; both members were immature, depressed, impulsive people. The joint business venture was not doing well, and Mrs. Alden was resentful and frightened by Mr. Samuels' irresponsibility. His bullying attitude dovetailed with her victimized position. Mr. Samuels' history revealed a lifetime of unstable relationships; Mrs. Alden's history was that of a 19-year-old mother, abandoned when her daughter was 2 months old, and subsequently totally dependent on her parents. She remarried at age 24, but her second husband left 5 years later. During this time, her parents continued to support her and Linda.

The couple sessions were chaotic and explosive as the couple attempted to delineate their needs. Further sessions revealed an abusive man who threatened suicide when Mrs. Alden talked about separation. Within several weeks, Mrs. Alden decided that she wanted to end the relationship. Mr. Samuels was furious with the therapists, refused the individual sessions offered to him, and left treatment. He became severely depressed, continued to threaten suicide, and refused to leave the apartment until the grandfather assisted Mrs. Alden in convincing him to leave.

Individual Sessions with Mother and Mother–Daughter Sessions

Mrs. Alden went into a moderately severe agitated depression, fearful that she would be the cause of Mr. Samuels' possible suicide and because he had failed her as a rescuer. Linda covered her terror of her mother's impotent stage by bragging that she had been the powerful person who had gotten rid of Mr. Samuels. She was furious at her mother "for being weak and dependent on him."

The next phase of treatment involved supportive therapy for Mrs. Alden and exploratory treatment with mother and Linda who had reversed roles. Mrs. Alden did not know how to structure or nurture her child, who was an extension of herself. This paralleled the symbiotic relationship between grandmother and Mrs. Alden. History revealed that the grandmother had been dependent on mood-elevating drugs and tranquilizers. She had given diet pills to her daughter during her early teenage years, so that she would not be fat like the oldest daughter. The grandmother's mother had died when she was 9 years old, and grandmother's sister had told her that grandmother was responsible for the death. Guilt over this accusation remained with grandmother and made her overanxious about her children's welfare. Grandmother's zealousness about her childrens' lives had prevented Mrs. Alden from the maturing experience of living with anxiety. She was treated as an infant whenever she would become anxious, and she felt utterly dependent on other people to save her, particularly men. She had poor recall of her teenage years other than her parent's goal that she should marry a rich, handsome knight in shining armor who would take care of her so that she would never suffer any pain. Any negative emotions by other people were seen as a reflection of herself, so she would double her efforts to try to please the other.

Although historically Catholic, religious affiliation was loose for family members. Treatment was a balancing act as Linda pushed for greater structuring from her mother. Linda's truancies from school increased as did revelations of delinquent activity. It was as if she were trying to provide mother with sufficient material to provide the structure that she needed. Mrs. Alden balked at parenting tasks, was furious with the therapists, and wanted to leave the child in the office. At this time, Linda was having brief individual sessions, 15-minute subsessions of the mother–child time. Because of the acting-out behavior, more individual work was considered, with Linda fighting all the way, saying that she did not know if she would be back for the next visit, but arriving on time, keeping her coat on, her books in her lap, jutting her jaw, and with a huge pout. Linda's defensive fortress began to erode as the therapist used the alter ego technique with her. She began to get furious with the therapists as they were not able to change her mother instantly.

Mrs. Alden required temporary antidepressants as she experienced her dependent roles diminishing. When the boutique business folded, she was able to secure her first real job. Her parents had been totally supporting her financially in exchange for her acceptance of their infantilization. A suspected problem of alcoholism with Mrs. Alden was further elucidated as Linda revealed her own alcohol dependency. This seemed to be the only way that she could bring her mother's drinking to the attention of the therapist. Mrs. Alden's isolation and loneliness from peer relationships became evident; her family had always filled the gap, instilling in her a severe distrust of the outside world. Because there were no appropriate groups at the agency, part of the treatment at this point was to be her involvement in a consciousness-raising group, which she resisted strongly. The highlight of this phase of the treatment was when her turn came to have the group in her home. She had never been a hostess for a social event, and her pride in herself and the boost in self-esteem had a ripple effect. Her horizons became broader; she explored other job opportunities.

Linda could allow her dependency needs to be more obvious as mother assumed more of an adult role. During this phase of treatment, Mrs. Alden wrote to Linda's father requesting financial help as she was determined to provide a private high school education for her daughter. He responded by providing financial help and also began writing to Linda. He then visited the city and agreed to several joint sessions with Linda and Mrs. Alden. By this time about 1 year had elapsed since the initial call.

Then grandmother called for treatment for herself, as her daughter, Mrs. Alden, was becoming healthier and moving away from her. Son Charles, involved with a woman he eventually married, left the maternal home. Grandmother was unhappy and lonely now that Mrs. Alden was more independent and that Linda was more involved with mother and decreasingly involved with her grandparents. Grandmother was seen for several sessions, all of which grandfather refused to join. After that, she stopped treatment. Grandmother was given antianxiety medication by her private physician. Mrs. Alden tried to have her enter treatment again, but she refused.

Linda and her mother paralleled in their development; both improved their peer relationships. Linda made a good adjustment to her new school, dissipating her previous antiauthority rampage. Mrs. Alden studied for, and became, a computer programmer. As her mother became more responsible, Linda could let her loneliness, fears of abandonment, and depression come through, sometimes requesting additional sessions during stressful times (e.g., breaking up with her boyfriend and her stepfather's reinvolvement with her in a quasiseductive fashion). The mother became the mother and the child, the child. Linda laughs about the way she used to be so tough; when so moved, she cries in sessions. Both have a growing network of friends; neither mother nor daughter are searching for the knights in shining armor. Mrs. Alden feels that she can manage both herself and Linda, has successfully gone through the mourning of the loss of her two previous husbands and the loss of the idealized parents, holds a responsible job, and is financially independent.

This case illustrates the use of the Rem family suprasystem initially and the whittling down that is done from the whole to the parts. In the initial telephone work, persistence and patience were necessary to set up the evaluation. It demonstrates how the cotherapy team was available to different sections of the suprafamily and how sabotage of treatment was avoided at the outset by involving the crucial grandfather.

Systems, insight producing, and behavioral approaches were employed and were invaluable for the outcome. The Rem unit originally was not viable, and its dissolution seemed to be necessary for the maturing and individuating process to take place in the mother. Linda originally had taken the role that many children of divorce and Rem do, of the pseudo-mature person who parents the parent. Although her father was not directly involved until a year later, his presence was made known by the systems approach, and his influence as a ghost was recognized. Because the first stepfather was approached but refused to be involved, he was also treated as an unpresent presence.

CONCLUSION

A great deal was reported in this article, an attempt to briefly explain the results of 5 years' work. As in all mental health areas, the prime concern must be prevention of distress and damage to people. What we have presented, although centered around theory and therapy, provides the underpinning for our prophylactic work.

Clinical work with this type of group of families can be rewarding. Even though the complexity of Rem can create problems, it also is the basis of the richness of relationships and experiences that such a family can provide to the individual, satisfying a need we all have for a variety of encounters and emotions. When we work with these families, we are attuned to both how they are alike and different from nuclear families. We attend to the Rem family suprasystem as well as the Rem family subsystem and include all people who have an impact on the current situation. We look at the family's development over time and take an eclectic approach emphasizing flexibility, understanding of behavioral and dynamic factors, goal-directed work, as well as the play of the therapist's own reactions in his or her intervention.

NOTES

1. Founded in 1976 by Clifford Sager, M.D., Director, this service is the Remarried Consultation Service of the Jewish Board of Family and Children's Services, New York, N.Y.
2. Between May 1977 and April 1979, 213 Rem families were treated in the agency. Data concerning these families are available in Crohn, Sager et al. Understanding and Treating the Child in the Remarried Family.
3. This work resulted in an annotated bibliography, by Walker, Brown, et al. (1979), and in a literature review: Sager et al. (1980).
4. A forthcoming book (Brunner/Mazel, 1982) will expand on our theoretical, clinical, and preventive approach.
5. The reader is advised to refer to Berman & Leif (1975) and Carter & McGoldrich (1980).

6. When a Rem couple requests help exclusively for their marital relationship, an ex-spouse may be seen conjointly with the new couple if it is indicated and if all three (or four) adults agree. If so, the agenda is limited to those items agreed upon in advance. Sometimes it is most helpful to have former spouses meet alone with the therapists to complete aspects of the emotional divorce. To do this requires that the therapist be alert to setting at ease the new spouse. If this is not possible, this option should be reconsidered.

7. For a complete explanation of genograms, see Guerin & Penagast (1976) or Brodt (1980).

REFERENCES

Berman, E.M., & Leif, H.I. Marital therapy from a psychiatric perspective: An overview. *American Journal of Psychiatry,* 1975, *132,* 583-592.

Brodt, J.O. *The family diagram.* Washington, D.C.: Groome Center, 1980.

Carter, E., & McGoldrich, M. *The family life cycle: A framework for family therapy.* New York: Gardner Press, 1980.

Crohn, H., Sager, C. et al. Understanding and treating the child in the remarried family. In *Children of separation and divorce.* New York: Van Nostrand Reinhold, 1981.

Guerin, P.J., & Penagast, E.G. Evaluation of family systems and genogram. *Family therapy: Theory and practice.* New York: Gardner Press, 1976.

Lacquer, P.P. Multiple family therapy. In Ferber, A. et al. *The book of family therapy.* Boston: Houghton Mifflin, 1972.

MacGregor, R. et al. *Multiple impact therapy with families.* New York: McGraw-Hill, 1964.

Messinger, L. Remarriage between divorced people with children from previous marriages: A proposal for preparation for remarriage. *Journal of Marriage and Family Counselling,* 1976, *2,* 193-200.

Sager, C.J. *Marriage contracts and couples therapy.* New York: Brunner/Mazel, 1976.

Sager, C.J. The psychotherapist's continuous evaluation of his work. *Psychoanalytic Review,* 1957, *44,* 298-312.

Sager, C.J., & Hunt, B. *Intimate partners—Hidden patterns in love relationships.* New York: McGraw-Hill, 1979.

Sager, C.J. et al. Remarriage revisited. *Family and Child Mental Health Journal,* 1980, *6,* 19-25.

Wynne, L.C. et al. Pseudomutuality in the family relations of schizophrenics. *Psychiatry,* 1958, *21,* 205-220.

12. Remarriage Family: Structure, System, Future

Virginia Goldner, Ph.D.
Formerly
Family Therapy Training Center
Philadelphia Child Guidance Clinic
Philadelphia, Pennsylvania
Currently
Albert Einstein College of Medicine
New York, New York

Twelve

REPORTS OF DEMOGRAPHIC TRENDS IN FAMILY LIFE HAVE made it increasingly clear that family therapy will have to stretch if it is to stay in touch with the social reality of current American life. Statistics on family relations demonstrate that the intact nuclear family is being steadily eclipsed by a collage of alternative kinship and household arrangements that by 1990 will characterize the majority of American families (Masnick & Bane, 1980).

These changes in the social organization of family life present a special kind of challenge to family therapists. Insofar as the techniques and basic theoretical assumptions grew out of a particular social ecology and a particular historical period that are rapidly receding into the past, one cannot complacently assume that the ideas and strategies developed within that special niche will be appropriate for the conditions of family life that characterize the present period.

The uncritical acceptance of traditional sex role arrangements by family therapists of the 1950s was a blind spot of limited clinical consequence, because it mirrored the reigning cultural assumptions of the time. But the same uncritical stance in the current context would be unacceptable, since the family is now being relentlessly challenged by conflicting ideologies about how gender relations should be structured. Similarly, family therapists can no longer lazily define so-called non-traditional families in terms of their deviance from the intact nuclear family, since that would mean making an aging, fading norm, the measure against which to evaluate the social arrangements that are taking its place.

189

To come to terms with current realities, family therapists need to incorporate an appreciation of the social evolution of family life within family therapy theory itself. From such a perspective, alternative kinship arrangements lose their status as deviant and emerge as new stages in a more complex family life cycle (Carter & McGoldrick, 1980). By extending the conception of family development to include single parenthood, remarriage, a change in sexual orientation, and any of a number of alternatives, we can begin to locate these life transitions within an unfolding process instead of isolating them from the social context that gives them meaning. This is, of course, the impulse of family therapists generally—to normalize rather than pathologize human experience.

But such a project does not mean merely tacking on new stages of life to keep up with social fashion. If the first marriage is no longer the happy ending to childhood, but rather the first in a series of stages that characterize a more demanding adult life, family therapists need to recast their understanding of family structure and development with this in mind. Clearly, the same factors that have led to the increases in divorce, single parenthood, and remarriage are also transforming the experience and meaning of life in the nuclear family as well.

THE REMARRIAGE FAMILY STRUCTURE

The need for a richer theoretical vocabulary to encompass the facts of family life in the 1980s can easily be illustrated by looking at the situation of the remarried family, a family type that is becoming increasingly common, since most divorces are followed by remarriage, and the divorce rate is fast approaching 50% (Glick, 1979). Since the remarried family is a product of the fractured remains of at least one, and sometimes more than one, family system, it cannot be understood apart from this elaborate developmental history—a history that can include two separate and parallel sequences of marriage, parenthood, separation, divorce, and single parenthood, followed by a second courtship. Moreover, since the family formed by remarriage is a hybrid of these previous kinship arrangements, its internal structure is far more complex than the family types from which it emerged. In this sense, the remarried family both contains and subsumes its intricate past.

Given such a complex social organism, the theoretical challenge is to build a conceptual framework tailored to this complex reality, rather than use one that reduces it to fit our anachronistic categories. Such a project is far more than an academic exercise, since the experience of family life is determined, to a large extent, by the social categories in which it operates. If these categories are arbitrary and restrictive, then people trying to live within them will feel pinched and cornered. Put another way, if the cultural definitions that shape family life do not fully apply to the remarried family, then people in these families will have great difficulty living out their ambiguous social status.

Listen to how members of two families, referred to the Philadelphia Child Guidance Clinic because of problems with their adolescent children, responded to Salvador Minuchin's question, "How do you see things in the family?"

Bill (father):	I don't feel comfortable in terms of a family . . . . I don't feel we're all together in anything. . . .It's a very uncomfortable situation for me in terms of a lack of closeness between all of us.
Eve (mother):	I would like us to have more "family feelings." There's more animosity now than when we were first married.
Minuchin:	Maybe that is a family feeling.
Eve:	(laughs) Maybe it is, but I'm not used to it. I didn't have it as a family feeling before, so I'm not ready to accept that as "just family."
Tom (Bill's son by first marriage):	How can I accept Eve's discipline of me? I cannot, she's a total stranger to me.
Pete (Eve's son from first marriage):	It's a house I live in, it's not a home. Home is a place where I think of the people being together. I didn't think of this as a home. I just thought of it as a house, where I stay.

And from a second family:

Louis (father):	We're just not close like we should be, that's the biggest problem. There's always one person coming up against the other . . . .

Donna (Louis'
daughter from
his first
marriage):   It's not a family, it's a group of people living together.
That's how I see it.

Sharon (Louis'
stepdaughter):   It's just not togetherness. Everyone is always argu-
ing with each other.

(Goldner & Minuchin, 1982)

Taken together, these comments reveal a peculiarly disquieting kind of complaint. Instead of responding to the therapist's query with the usual problems presented by families in crisis, these people seem to be burdened by something much more fundamental. They are facing a crisis of legitimacy in which their identity as a family is in question. It is this underlying identity crisis that paralyzes them, not the specific conflicts that brought them into treatment.

What is at issue here is more than the lack of fit between the outdated images of family life promulgated by the culture and the more complex realities of that life within the remarried family. Puncturing the illusion that normal families are organized on the "Ozzie and Harriet" model typical of the 1950s is an essential bit of consciousness raising, but it is only a partial antidote to the experience of alienation that colors the inner life of these families.

A brief review of normal family development illustrates why. Intact families function like tiny insulated cultures. They develop transactional patterns that operate like social norms, regulating how the business of daily life will be conducted. These rules of organization shape the most elemental human experiences of mind, self, body, and relations to others, and provide the stability and continuity necessary for the integrity of the family system. Complex interlocking feedback mechanisms maintain the transactional sequences the family has developed, so that they survive, like traditions in any self-contained society, long after their origins are lost. If one observes a family long enough, these sequences can be isolated and even predicted before they recur.

This circular, repetitive internal structure is one of the defining features of family life, and provides the rationale for the de-emphasis of the past in much of family treatment. The argument, briefly, is that disturbed behavior in one family member is embedded in an ongoing repetitive transactional pattern that involves the whole family. Thus, a change in the individual requires a change in the rules that organize this repetitive sequence. The original cause of the symptomatology is no longer relevant.

To emphasize the power of present transactions in their context over past experiences is, however, to presume certain conditions of family life that absolutely do not apply to the remarried family. Intact families develop their circular, repetitive, inner structure because the people in those families share a common past and live with the expectation of a common future. The redundancy that so characterizes family relations depends on the passage of time, since these repeating sequences of interaction are nothing more exotic than transactional ruts that develop a kind of functional autonomy as the family drifts into coalitions and necessary subsystems differentiate their functions.

Thus, history can be dismissed as a significant factor in intact families precisely because history prevails. It is, in fact, the weight of history, the sense of going on and on together that distinguishes family relations from all other social arrangements. This experience of continuity gives meaning to the phrase *blood ties*—the reality of an unbreakable web of relationships that persists no matter how the individuals feel about one another. It is what Robert Frost captured in the line "home is the place where, when you have to go there, they have to take you in."

Clearly, none of these conditions apply to the remarried family. Only some members of the new family share a common history. Custody and living arrangements for children who may be active members in two family systems, sometimes even shuttling between two households, produce uncertainty about the future.

Being cut loose from the moorings that typically secure the unassailable sense of continuity that we associate with family life has powerful consequences for the sense of family in remarried families. Lacking a common culture in which to locate their own identity and their experience with one another, it is no wonder that relationships feel arbitrary and false, indeed that nothing feels quite right. It is an as-if situation in which roles have been assigned, but persons have been somehow ignored.

What should be clear by now is that blending two families is an inherently disorganizing experience that involves the total transformation of the individuals' intimate world. The emotional traditions that construct the familiar redundancy of family relations concern the most intimate, private, and seemingly trivial details of daily life, which are ordinarily hidden from the public world. Bathroom habits, food preferences, sleep rituals—the most private, primitive aspects of being human—provide the material for the interpersonal encounters out of which individual identity and family structure develop. To borrow a concept from anthropology, families transform physical facts (like walking, eating, and elimination), into social and psychological realities. They transform nature into culture. Thus, to move from an intact nuclear family system into a different kinship arrangement can tear apart all of the rituals of private life that make the world feel orderly and natural and that maintain, invisibly, a stable internal experience of self. Instead of being embedded in a context, one is drifting self-consciously, in an ambiguous, poorly articulated field. The new context is as disorienting as having to think about how to walk while trying to walk or to think about how to make love while trying to make love.

Even though there is nothing in family systems theory that would deny the foregoing analysis, there is also little to illuminate it. The habit of mind that orients thinkers about family systems to focus on the rule-governed aspects of the present context and to mistrust forays into the past can blind the therapist to the fundamental existential crisis facing the remarried family: that there are no rules organizing their intimate family system. Family members are not all dancing to the same music because the melody line has been fractured. Indeed, if the remarried family is to get beyond the critical problems of this initial period, it will have to orchestrate, collaboratively, a new, more complex set of harmonics for its internal relations. Such a project is, in fact, the initial developmental task facing all families at the remarriage stage of the life cycle. It is also the initial clinical challenge facing the family therapist who works with them.

DEVELOPMENTAL TASKS OF REMARRIAGE FAMILY

So what can be done? If the special intimacies of the nuclear family depend on its social isolation and unbroken ties with the past, then how are members of a remarried family ever to shake off the collective sensation that their so-called family is, in comparison, nothing more than an arbitrary charade? It is not enough to counsel such families to give up wanting what they cannot have. People remarry and form second families precisely because they want the experience of family, an image loaded down with particular meanings. As our case study informants told us, a family is far more than a household. For Donna that distinction was stark and simple. "We're not a family," she said, "we're a bunch of people living together." For Pete, who captured the contrast in metaphor, it was "a house I live in, but not a home."

And here lies the ingredients of a paradox. Because remarried households do not feel like home, nothing that occurs within them will be seen as real; therefore, there is little commitment to building family relationships.

The knot that ties everyone's hand depends upon a mental construction that frames the family's current experience as false. This presumption is a consequence of various aspects of the family's circumstances, some of which have already been described—the most important being the lack of a common history and therefore a common culture. Since this is a fact of life, and not a state of mind, it is not immediately apparent that there is any role for psychotherapy to play here. Yet if one looks a bit closer, it begins to seem as if it is not only the past itself that is missing for these families but a sense of the past. When people meet in adult life and form important relationships, they slowly accumulate a feeling for the other's past history. Spouses who did not grow up together nevertheless develop a rich set of images regarding their mate's past life. Intimacy invites a kind of empathic imagination that can include a mental picture of someone's boyhood or girlhood, the dead grandparents, old friends, past lovers, and simply, a sense of what it was like at home for those we love. These mental images are essential to a family's sense of context, both historical and current. Thus the question emerges: What has blocked the operation of simple curiosity in these families and interrupted what could be an effortless process of acquiring the sense of a shared history?

Moreover, the argument regarding the feelings of alienation that result from these families' lack of a common past begins to erode from the moment they set up housekeeping together. By the end of the first day, their common past has begun. The issue, therefore, is not simply time itself, but the ability of the family to use the effects of time in the service of its own development. Think again about the self reports of the two families whose comments began this section. Their level of alienation makes them sound like people who could not have been together more than a few months; yet, in fact, both households have been functioning for over 3 years. So a similar question emerges: what has interfered with the developmental process in these families that typically keeps pace with the passage of time?

A family with a 3-year history should have an internal structure that reflects 3 years of development. It should have evolved a culture that gives its members the feeling of belonging to something personal. It should have differentiated itself into a variety of internal subsystems, each with distinct functions and boundaries, and all integrated into the larger family system. In short, like an individual, a family must grow with time, becoming more internally complex as life's demands accelerate.

But the families we have been looking at do not seem to have aged in this way. Their subjective experience of alienation is an accurate reflection of their underdeveloped structure, which has remained primitive despite the march of time. It is as if the developmental clock had frozen after a few months, leaving them inadequately equipped to handle the tasks of later life.

To understand what keeps these families from moving forward, it is necessary to understand what they are up against. In a sense, all remarried families are faced with an impossible developmental challenge. They must accomplish the task of forming a family. At the same time, they must function like a family further along in the family life cycle. In other words, they must operate as if they had developed the complex inner structure of a family who has been together at least as long as the age of the oldest child while actually possessing only the rudimentary structure of a family just starting out. In short, they must function at two stages of the life cycle at once.

This creates all kinds of contradictory trajectories, since it means that the developmental needs of the family as a whole may be in conflict with the developmental needs of the individuals who comprise it. This contradiction is most severe in remarried families who come together when their children are teenagers. At this juncture, the maturational tasks of adolescence, which involve challenging the family culture and beginning the process of separation from it, are in direct conflict with the developmental tasks of the new family, who must pull together precisely to create that culture. As a result, the adolescent is left with nothing to push against, and the family is left without the participation necessary to develop itself.

There is, therefore, no way for remarried families to avoid a period of profound disequilibrium, since family formation cannot be willed. It is an evolutionary process that develops at the rate at which real life presents its challenges. It takes time, for example, for spouses to develop a culture of two—to establish rules regarding sequences of contact and distance, sexuality, conflict expression and resolution, and so on. Similarly, it takes time for spouses to organize themselves as parents of infants, and later of toddlers, school-age children, and adolescents. And, by the same token, it takes time for children to organize themselves as siblings—to establish hierarchies of control and nurturance that reflect birth order relationships, to develop rules regarding areas of autonomy and subordination in relation to parents, and so on. But in a remarried family, there is no time for such structures to develop. All at once a single woman becomes a mother of three, or a child moves from the younger of two to the eldest of four.

The disruptive effects of these arbitrary rearrangements in a family's internal structure are further amplified when the new family members try to read one another. They cannot lean on the effortless familiarity that comes from time and physical proximity. Just sharing a household with an emotionally distant father, for example, provides easy access to all kinds of humble and intimate details about the man's character and habits that are invisible to the outside world. No matter how emotionally distant the father is, he is a known quantity to the household (he must be avoided in the early morning, but can be sought out after dinner).

Families absorb this sort of data about one another by osmosis. The data lose something in the translation, even to a family therapist, yet must be learned, often through painful and humiliating trial and error, as the remnants of two old family systems try to integrate themselves into some new kind of kinship structure.

Given the enormity of the developmental task at hand and of the intense and dislocating feelings that necessarily accompany it, the clinical mystery is not why some families falter and freeze up but why and how others succeed and continue to grow. We have, of course, only minimal data on the developmental course of the normal (nonclinical) remarried family.

For those families who do get stuck, however, the developmental perspective provides a framework from which to analyze the nature of their difficulty. In general, research on the process of remarriage indicates that it takes about 2 years for a remarried family to stabilize, developing a coherent sense of itself via internal rules, traditions, and subsystems, and also developing viable rules regarding relations with noncustodial parents and with siblings living with ex-spouses (Visher & Visher, 1979).

These data are enormously useful because, like normative descriptions of child development, they help to distinguish between the normal growing pains of remarried family life and the dysfunctional social arrangements of those families in need of help. It means, for example, that during the first 2 years of the remarriage the as-if experience is inevitable, and, therefore, complaints about a sense of falseness from any (or all) family members are to be expected. Similarly, resistance to developing an integrated family structure, as reflected in a child's unwillingness to yield to the discipline of a stepparent or in the constant eruptions of conflict between new siblings (to name just a few common problems), is to be interpreted as an appropriate response to the normal developmental crisis that all remarried families face at the outset of this life stage.

Indeed, the best advice to a family stumbling through the early phases of a remarriage can be lifted right out of the popular textbooks on surviving adolescence—"be patient, 'pass' on the small confrontations in order to keep the major issues in focus, and have faith that the outcome will have been worth all the turmoil."

After the first 2 years, however, the family should present itself quite differently. It should have established some kind of identity, which would necessarily include a sense of its own legitimacy as a family unit. Relationships between members of the two original family systems should be real but not necessarily close, and the boundary around the household unit should be sufficiently elastic that it can expand and contract to accommodate relationships with noncustodial parents and visiting siblings.

DYSFUNCTIONAL REMARRIAGE FAMILY STRUCTURE

In the families who have not achieved this level of organization, the complaints of the earlier period will probably persist. The initial therapeutic task, therefore, is to locate the impasse that prevents the family from proceeding with its development.

Although there are innumerable potential roadblocks to a successful remarriage, this argument will focus on one core concept borrowed from Watzlawick and his colleagues at the Mental Research Institute (Watzlawick, Weakland, & Fisch, 1974). The families who get stuck can be said to have developed a dysfunctional solution to the initial developmental trauma of the remarriage. It is this pseudosolution that keeps them mired.

There are two losing strategies that are particularly common. One is characterized by futile attempts, usually on the part of the parents, to manufacture a sense of togetherness, as if, by force of will, they could recreate the lost intimacies of the nuclear family. Not surprisingly, this pressure to invent a family only exaggerates the feelings of alienation and falseness that already permeate the atmosphere of the new household. At the other extreme are the families who seem to actively resist the process of blending together at all, thus creating a boarding-house environment in which the two sides share a household but never build a home.

Each of these dysfunctional scenarios suggests something different about the internal structure of the family system that produced it. In the first case, the family characterized by a "let us pretend" ethos, the marital subsystem is often solid, but the relationships between the parents and children, and within the sibling subsystem generally, are typically uneasy and distant. In the second case, the family that never blends, it is almost certain that the spouses have never developed a genuine bond between them. As both a cause and a consequence, each spouse has remained closer to his or her biological children than to the spouse, thus operating as two single-parent families living under one roof.

All kinds of problems can surface in families organized along either of these lines, but one common complaint seems to be the lack of any effective mechanism for resolving conflict. This is not surprising, since in both of these family types, the family is divided against itself.

This is obvious in the case of the family that refuses to blend. Here, dysfunctional coalitions along old family lines prevent the development of a viable executive subsystem between the new couple. Since they are pulled apart by their old attachments, they cannot function collaboratively as parents, and, as a consequence, the family is left leaderless and adrift. With no final court of appeals for the adjudication of disputes, the two parallel factions can be triggered into sequences of *symmetrical* escalation, leading eventually to the explosive annihilation of the family itself or (a likely step along the way) to the development of a pattern of deflection in which the flare-up of some kind of symptom puts a momentary stop to the relentless countdown.

By contrast, the *pseudomutual* (desperately happy) family divides along different lines. Here the split is not between the two original family systems, but between the two generations. In fact, one way to contrast these two fragile family structures is to specify the axis along which the central fissure develops. In the actively resistant family, division takes place along the vertical axis, leaving two parallel factions trapped under one roof. In the pseudomutual family, it is the horizontal axis that marks the split, with the happy parents foisting their fantasies on their appropriately angry and ambivalent children.

The outcome in this second case can often be a war between the generations characterized by *complimentary* escalation. As the children resist joining their parents' happy family, the parents respond by increasing their demands for proximity and identification with the family unit, thus triggering more extreme forms of withdrawal by the children. If the cycle is not interrupted by the development of a symptom, then some kind of structural collapse can be the result. Since the parents remain committed to the new family (or more accurately, to their fantasy of a new family), it is usually the children who leave the field, either moving in with the noncustodial parent, or if they are old enough, simply leaving home prematurely.

This outcome is unfortunate and unnecessary because these families, given some guidance, can probably develop into viable kinship systems. The prognosis is less favorable for the resistant family type because the relationship between the spouses is so marginal. Success can be achieved, however, if family members can learn to function in this highly complex, ambiguous social field. This, in turn, depends on their ability to recognize that membership in a blended family only complicates the previous kinship context; it does not replace it.

This applies especially to the children of such families, who must negotiate a more complex network of relationships than their parents. They may, for example, be active members of two different family systems, sometimes even shuttling between two households on different days of the week. Their family experience differs profoundly from that of the parents, since it varies as a function of their location in the maze of interconnected family units that constitute the kinship network of remarriage.

Given such elaborate social arrangements and the delicate alliances, loyalty conflicts, and conflicting subcultures that must be mastered, it is not possible for a child to simply join the new family unit, closing the door on the rest of his or her context. Moreover, it is a dangerous and highly inflammatory oversimplification for parents to make such a demand, since it will inevitably activate resistance and countermaneuvers, not only in the child but in the rest of the kinship system as well.

Within the newly formed household unit, this conflict can surface as a struggle between past and present. The parents say, in effect, "Deny the past, make this your family now," and the children counter by holding themselves back from entering the family at all, thus negating the present altogether. This kind of stalemate strangles the new family because it cannot grow into a complex organism without incorporating a sense of history into its current reality while its members are still struggling over its right to exist.

All of these dysfunctional scenarios can be understood as particular instances of what now can be stated as a general principle. Crises that paralyze remarried families are ultimately rooted in fundamental questions of family identity that can be traced back to fundamental problems with family development. This formulation then translates into a clinical strategy in which the goal of treatment is to foster the development of a genuine family identity by facilitating alternative solutions to the developmental impasse that has impeded family formation.

For the most part, this task does not require any special therapeutic techniques. The crucial issue is to understand the unique developmental demands facing this kind of family, and then to clarify how, in each particular case, the current structure of family relations is impeding that process. Once this has become clear, the project of changing the family depends on the usual mix of talent, mutual good will, and serendipity.

THERAPEUTIC TECHNIQUES FOR REMARRIAGE FAMILIES

There is, however, a particular kind of resistance to the therapeutic process that is peculiar to remarried families, which seems to be activated by the conditions of the therapeutic situation. Insofar as therapy invites, indeed requires, that families observe themselves, it exaggerates the feelings of self-consciousness that these families find so alienating and therefore try to avoid. Moreover, since family members expect (wrongly) that relations between them should feel natural, they resist any suggestion that building a second family requires self-conscious collaboration.

To manage this kind of resistance to getting started, it is essential that these underlying assumptions be elicited and challenged at the outset. A delay in this initial confrontation may jeopardize the authenticity of the therapeutic experience because the family may go along with the therapist's suggestions while never actually making a commitment to the process. This will only increase their feelings of alienation and their conviction that the whole effort is a sham.

But beyond a challenge to the family's naive and inaccurate assumptions, the therapist can confront the issue of authenticity directly and experientially. As has already been described, the feelings of falseness that plague these families can be traced back to the lack of a common history out of which a sense of family identity and culture develop. Therapy can provide a unique opportunity for these families to both acquire a past and deal with the internal conflicts that so far have prevented it.

A surprisingly effective and economical clinical strategy is to ask family members to exchange memories of the past. When and how this is framed, and to whom, are matters of individual clinical judgment and imagination. But no matter what the circumstances, the impact of this seemingly mild intervention is often unexpectedly powerful. Stepsiblings who may have appeared to be permanently estranged can find themselves in an animated discussion comparing notes about their parents' courtship or about how things changed for each of them in the moves from a nuclear family, to a single-parent family, to a remarried family. Similarly, parents who may have been locked into a position of defensive denial when faced with their children's past resentments can easily drift into reminiscing about how difficult it was for them to handle the divided loyalties and conflicting agendas sparked by their remarriage.

It is often the tiny details that break the ice. Pete, for instance, the adolescent who characterized his new family as ''a house I live in, not a home'' talked about his memories of the early months of his mother's remarriage in a later session.

Mom may not have noticed it, but in the beginning there was a change. Like the way we used to kid at home. I was used to that but Bill and Tom (stepfather and brother) didn't do it. So we went from a very *open* family to not very open, and I drifted away I guess.

Later in the same session Tom, Pete's stepbrother, used Pete's memories as a link back into his own. Turning to his father, he was now able to say:

I thought you wanted me to adjust. To change over to Eve's (stepmother) rules. Like when my bedtime got changed, that was traumatic. I thought we were adapting to Eve's ways. I didn't feel we were combining the two.

These bits of memorabilia contain fragments from the lost past of both families and document how that past was denied in the attempt to invent a new family. Clearly, both of these boys experienced the parental pressure to accommodate to the new family, not as a four-way collaboration but as a betrayal of their own family's subculture and as a triumph for the culture of the other side. If the family is ever to build an authentic family identity, it will have to integrate, not negate, the two family subcultures, which means dealing with the experience of betrayal.

Many families avoid this reckoning because they fear destabilizing the clearly fragile status quo. But if they get beyond their initial resistance to facing the past, the process can develop a momentum of its own. This is because in the act of sorting through old memories the family has begun to excavate its common heritage. Everyone in a remarried family has lived through a similar upheaval and can understand, far better than any outside professional, how painful and disorienting the experience of re-marriage can be. As family members come to identify with one another's pain, they can no longer hold each other responsible for it. This marks the beginning of their growing up.

We can see this progression from divisive recrimination to mutual support in Donna, the adolescent who began treatment with the observation, "this isn't a family, it's a bunch of people living together." By the fifth session, she is trying to help a younger stepsibling cope with her despair about her father's infrequent visits since his own remarriage. "My brother and I know what you're going through," Donna says, "we've had practice with pain."

In bringing the family together to exchange pieces of the past, the therapist activates an integrative process that is necessary for the development of an authentic family identity. There seem to be three phases to that process, which form their own developmental sequence. First, the family is presented with the task of building a common history by sharing memories of the past. This requires coming to terms with that past in the context of the present, which constitutes a second developmental mile-stone. And finally, both of these processes trigger a third—the activation of the family's own inner resources. As the authentic issues that have been avoided are addressed, family members' feelings of being trapped by one another yield to an expanded sense of possibility. Instead of reducing each other to cardboard roles, family members can now become three-dimensional persons, and through that transformation they can be gin to use one another to create a common culture.

Thus, for remarried families, a focus on the past can potentiate a leap into the future. This clinical strategy can be likened to the creation of a bonding ritual, or rite of passage, which consolidates and authenticates the new family unit.

THE SOCIAL CONTEXT OF REMARRIAGE

Throughout this article the experience of remarriage has been characterized as a normal developmental stage in an increasingly complex family life cycle. This attempt, however, has not been entirely successful because the picture of remarriage that emerges in these pages is distorted by a one-sided emphasis on dysfunction. If, as has been painstakingly argued in the preceding discussion, remarried families are to be seen as legitimate kinship arrangements and not as deviant, or even alternative, family types, then they cannot be defined solely in terms of their deficits. Moreover, since changing family forms are best understood as necessary and positive responses to changing social conditions, remarried families, far from being victims of their circumstances, must represent some kind of progressive social adaptation.

This speculation grows increasingly credible when one reviews the now familiar criticisms leveled at the nuclear family in recent years. Its small size and social isolation are frequently cited as problematic, since family members are often left with inadequate social supports in times of stress and the excessively intense and overcharged family relationships that family therapists call enmeshment seem to be promoted.

By contrast, remarriage provides families with the opportunity to appropriate a new set of kin who can provide a cushion when trouble arises and an alternative set of experiences when relationships run aground. Moreover, it can be argued that the mere presence of "difference" that comes from the addition of new people with different relationship styles is, in itself, a stimulus for improved family functioning. It is a familiar formulation of family systems theory that families must develop increasingly complex patterns of internal organization if they are to remain adaptive to the continuously changing maturational needs of their members and to a continuously changing environment. But if a family is socially isolated—as enmeshed nuclear families tend to be—its development can be retarded because the family lacks new information to stimulate internal growth. In retreating from environmental challenge, enmeshed families rigidify; they do not grow.

For the remarried family, retreat from the outside world is impossible because the outside is now within. Moreover, survival itself depends on the capacity of two groups of outsiders to transcend their narrow interests in order to create one common kinship system. To accomplish this transformation, the two subgroups must integrate their differences, not deny them as enmeshed families do. If they succeed, they will have produced, by necessity, a sturdy, complex, highly differentiated social organism. If they fail, the family may not survive at all. Even though nuclear families can remain quite primitive and still linger on, survival of a remarried family may well require a leap into complexity.

Given the enormous potential of remarriage to propel this kind of evolutionary leap in family organization, it is important to understand why the progressive aspects of remarriage are so rarely seen. Part of the problem, as has been suggested earlier, is that we are living in a transitional period in which the social organization of family life is changing more quickly than the cultural images and rituals that give it meaning. Because the legitimacy and comfort of family relations depend on custom and ritual, the effect of this lack of fit on remarried families has been to promote a retreat from complexity. In a fruitless attempt to recreate the experience of a nuclear family, these second families succeed only in caricaturing its limitations, at the expense of denying a more authentic, and potentially more highly evolved, family form. Not surprisingly, this denial and distortion of social reality is echoed in the culture at large. It can be detected in the current nostalgia for traditional cultural forms—for the days when men were men, women were women, and families were intact.

This pervasive mood of cultural retrenchment sharpens the contradictions for all families that deviate from the 1950s mode. But the problem is most acute for middle-class families, since the preeminence of the socially isolated nuclear family has never extended beyond the white middle class. In other segments of the society, where more fluid family forms have been the norm, the experience of remarriage is mediated by a host of traditions. Among poor black families, for example, there is even a social convention that legitimizes roles and expectations among people not related by blood. It is called "fictive kin" by the anthropologists, and "going for brothers" (or sisters) by the people themselves. Moreover, financial and child care responsibilities, which among middle-class remarried families, are usually arenas of struggle and disorder, are formalized throughout the extended kinship system of poor blacks, so that the vicissitudes of romantic love notwithstanding, domestic constancy can be secured (Stack, 1974).

Set against these examples, the dislocation and confusion that seem to be inevitable aspects of the remarriage experience can now be more properly seen as inevitable consequences of the breakdown of an intermediate social domain between the nuclear family and the larger society. As more and more couples divorce, it will become increasingly urgent to revive some kind of intermediate zone between the intensely private world of the family and the totally alienated public world. In the last analysis, it may not be the breakdown of the family that we all need to lament but the breakdown of the community that once enveloped it.

REFERENCES

Carter, E.A., & McGoldrick, M. *The family life cycle: A framework for family therapy.* New York: Gardner Press, 1980.

Glick, P.C. The future of the American family in current population reports. *Special Studies Series* (Publication No. P-23, 78). Washington, D.C.: U.S. Government Printing Office, 1979.

Goldner, V., & Minuchin, S. Just a house—not a home. Philadelphia: Philadelphia Child Guidance Clinic, 1982. (Videotape with commentary)

Masnick, G., & Bane, M.J. *The Nation's Families: 1960–1990.* Cambridge: Joint Center for Urban Studies, 1980.

Stack, C. *All our kin: Strategies for survival in a black community.* New York: Harper & Row, 1974.

Visher, E.B., & Visher, J.S. *Stepfamilies: A guide to working with stepparents and stepchildren.* New York: Brunner/Mazel, 1979.

Watzlawick, P., Weakland, J., & Fisch, R. *Change: Principles of problem formation and problem resolution.* New York: Norton, 1974.

SW